BLOOD ON THE RAZOR WIRE

A PRISON MEMOIR

BLOOD ON THE RAZOR WIRE

A PRISON MEMOIR

CHAD MARKS

Cover design by Ivica Jandrijevic
Interior layout and design by www.writingnights.org
Book preparation by Chad Robertson
Edited by Chad Robertson

ISBN: ###-###-#######
LIBRARY OF CONGRESS CATALOGING-IN-PUBLICATION DATA:
NAMES: Marks, Chad, author
TITLE: Blood on the Razor Wire – A Prison Memoir / Chad Marks
DESCRIPTION: Independently Published, 2020
IDENTIFIERS: ISBN ### (Perfect bound) |
SUBJECTS: | Non-Fiction | Prison | True Crime | Memoir | Gangs
CLASSIFICATION: Pending
LC record pending

Independently Published
Printed in the United States of America.
Printed on acid-free paper.

Although the author and publisher have made every effort to ensure that the
information in this book was correct at press time, neither author nor publisher assumes
any liability to any party for any loss, damage, or disruption caused by errors or
omissions, whether such errors or omissions result from negligence, accident,
or any other cause. Both author and publisher hereby disclaim any liability to any party.
Readers should contact their attorney
to obtain advice before pursuing any course of action.

Nothing is intended or should be interpreted as expressing or representing the views of
the U.S. Bureau of Prisons or any other department or agency of any government body.

24 23 22 21 20 9 8 7 6 5 4 3 2 1

DEDICATION

To my mother who has been there for me since the day I was born,
August 17, 1978. I love you more than I could say in words.

To my sister Monique, thank you for being you
and pushing me forward when I felt like giving up.

EPIGRAPH OR BLANK

A good plan, violently executed now,
is better than a perfect plan next week.
— Lt. General George Patton

CONTENTS

DEDICATION V
CONTENTS VII
ACKNOWLEDGEMENTS IX

PROLOGUE 1
CHAPTER ONE 3
CHAPTER TWO 13
CHAPTER THREE 15
CHAPTER FOUR 25
CHAPTER FIVE 29
CHAPTER SIX 38
CHAPTER SEVEN 41
CHAPTER EIGHT 51
CHAPTER NINE 57
CHAPTER TEN 65
CHAPTER ELEVEN 67
CHAPTER TWELVE 71
CHAPTER THIRTEEN 78
CHAPTER FOURTEEN 81
CHAPTER FIFTEEN 87
CHAPTER SIXTEEN 94
CHAPTER SEVENTEEN 101
CHAPTER EIGHTEEN 106
CHAPTER NINETEEN 109
CHAPTER TWENTY 116
CHAPTER TWENTY-ONE 120
CHAPTER TWENTY-TWO 131
CHAPTER TWENTY-THREE 138
CHAPTER TWENTY-FOUR 146
CHAPTER TWENTY-FIVE 154
CHAPTER TWENTY-SIX 167
CHAPTER TWENTY-SEVEN 180
CHAPTER TWENTY-EIGHT 187
CHAPTER TWENTY-NINE 192
CHAPTER THIRTY 194
CHAPTER THIRTY-ONE 198
CHAPTER THIRTY-TWO 207
CHAPTER THIRTY-THREE 214

CHAPTER THIRTY-FOUR...216
CHAPTER THIRTY-FIVE...221
CHAPTER THIRTY-SIX..229
CHAPTER THIRTY-SEVEN...234
CHAPTER THIRTY-EIGHT...236
CHAPTER THIRTY-NINE..239
CHAPTER FORTY..242
EPILOGUE..243

ABOUT THE AUTHOR..245

ACKNOWLEDGEMENTS

A big thank you to Lisa Jacobi at Freedom Fighters, without you this book would not have been possible. I am forever grateful for you and the way you fought for my Freedom. Freedom with a capital F. Where would I be without your compassion, hard work, and dedication?

A special thank you to Amy Ralston-Povah at CAN-DO Clemency Foundation who broke her back trying to get me out of prison under President Obama's Clemency initiative. Although we were not successful we fought like hell, and I will be forever grateful to you.

To my brothers and sisters locked up, who live and fight in this struggle in their long walk to freedom.

To those who lost their lives to senseless violence in the Federal Bureau of Prisons, you're never forgotten.

Last, but not least, to the victims of crimes throughout the world, your pain will never be forgotten.

PROLOGUE

"THE COURT MUST ALSO consider the seriousness of the offense. And I think forty years—the statutory minimum by my calculation—reflects that seriousness. You're now twenty-four years of age. Even with good time, you will be into your sixties when and if you are released.

"Guided by the statute that says I must impose a sentence sufficient—and I think in this context if a sentence of forty years is not sufficient to comport with the statute, I'm not sure what is. So that's the sentence I intend to impose."

That's precisely what he said. Those were his exact words. A Federal District Judge who, with the swing of his gavel, made it final on a cold March 2003 afternoon in Rochester, New York. All my dreams, desires and hopes had been stamped out. Forty years in the Federal Bureau of Prisons for drug dealing—low level drug dealing. I'm sure I'm not the only person who thought only killers and rapists received those types of sentences. That day I found out I was wrong.

I am being led from the courtroom. I look back to see my mother crying. I read her lips. "I love you Chad." I taste the salt from the first teardrop running down my face. I feel the clamps of the cold, metal, handcuffs bite my skin. My mother disappears. I wonder to myself if that will be the last time I ever see her...

CHAPTER

ONE

THINGS CAN BE REALLY DEVIANT in this world. I am transported into a limbo realm. Chained up from head to toe, I am forced to withstand being flung through the atmosphere with other redundant looking creatures of all nationalities. We're prisoners now. Although we are human beings, we are no longer part of civilized society—no longer part of that equation. My destination is some concrete jungle—USP Big Sandy. I've heard many rumors about how foul and dangerous this place is. Many say that it is the worst prison in the Federal Bureau of Prisons. Beatings, stabbings, and death occur there on a regular basis. I guess the rumors I heard when I was younger—that federal prison is Camp Fed—were wrong.

Now that I know what I know, oh, how I wish they'd been true.

THE KNOCK ON THE CELL DOOR did not wake me, but it scared me.

"Marks, pack up! You're leaving in half an hour."

The inevitable is here. I am leaving this private prison holding center.

I've been waiting for this moment for months. I'm heading to the real big house. I do not want to answer the correctional officer, so I keep my head on the pillow.

"Marks! You up?"

"I got you man, I got you. I'm up."

"I'll be back in twenty minutes. Be ready."

I drag myself from beneath the thin, grey-white sheets. The blanket must have fallen to the floor in the restless night. I kick the blanket to the side and wipe the crust from the corners of my eyes. The cold water I splash on my face wakes me. The light comes on and the other residents of this cell—the mice—scuttle for cover.

I stare into the mirror at the face that always looks back at me. I watch tears. Loneliness. I watch fear and desperation roll slowly down my face. My emotions are at a picnic. My face is the venue. I have finally come face-to-face with reality. I am on my way to a real prison to begin serving my very real prison sentence. Cold water on my face again. I mouth the words, "You're going to be alright no matter what."

My reflection does no more than stare back. Before long I am led out to the R&D Department like a package being trussed for shipping. The only difference is my packaging is not cardboard, rather shackles, handcuffs, and chains.

After enduring some lengthy mental, and physical torture in what is called the U.S. Marshall's Transportation Service, I am taken from the private prison in Youngstown, Ohio and thrown into a medieval place called USP Atlanta. The prison is located in the Atlanta, Georgia inner-city. Many of the men I am now forced to co-exist with in here seem to be creatures of violence. Angry men. Men who want to share their hatred with everyone they meet. I must go through this transportation process in order to get to my final destination, that far off concrete jungle in the Blue Grass State—Big Sandy. The real big house. Inez, Kentucky, here I come.

I cannot wait for this trip to be over with, I think to myself. But perhaps I am safer here? I mumble softly. No one else can hear me. The feelings engulf me, and my desperate eyes scan the battle-scarred faces of the other men. So many thrive on creating misery for others, misery on a scale that would make Purgatory jealous. My mind drifts again. I am wondering why they thrive on suffering, on wreaking it on others. I am among prisoners. Bottled up violence ready to unleash on those around them.

I find myself in a gauntlet of disgrace and terror. I am dazed. I am crammed into a nine-by-nine shithole. I am surrounded by six slabs of non-penetrable solid matter. USP Atlanta is a ghettoized concrete jungle where a normal person cannot distinguish guard from inmate, except by the clothing they wear.

This Atlanta prison is the home of the infamous November 1987, Cuban riots. The riots resulted in a large part of the prison being burnt to the ground. Those acts of rebellion and rioting cost millions of taxpayer dollars. The riot lasted eleven days, during which time inmates took over a hundred hostages. After the smoke cleared, and the riot was extinguished, all the Cuban inmates were transported to Leavenworth Penitentiary in Kansas. Once in Kansas, the Cubans were locked in cells for twenty-four hours a day, seven days a week. It was not Dorothy's kind of Kansas. This Kansas left many men wondering why they ever fled Fidel Castro's Cuba and his evil regime. No place like home, no longer sounded so bad. But tapping shoes and a few words would not take away their newfound anguish.

USP Atlanta now houses inmates in a general population section of the prison. Another portion of the prison is used as a transportation hub. This is where I am placed. This is where prisoners, like me, wait to be transported to misery and pain. They send us to that unflattering part of life by plane or bus. Atlanta here I am. There's no Magic City strip club. There are no women shaking their asses. That's in the distance. Right now, right here is simple concrete, steel, and violence I suppose, for the next forty years. If I make it that long.

The correctional officer leads me to my temporary cell. Another person is already inside; he looks more like a homeless man than a convict. I am forced to share this little area of misery with another dysfunctional man. I'm supposed to call this man my cell-mate, or "cellie." The two of us are crammed into this shithole. It smells like hell and is riddled with filth and graffiti. As I scan the walls I read aloud. "Fuck the Feds" and "God Save Me" are scribbled next to other assorted vulgarity. Hell of a contrast, I think. A small smile creeps in like a looming ghost. Two different points of view from two different people. Perhaps the same person authored both. Sad, confused, angry, and desolate, I wish God or Jesus Christ would save me too.

My cell-mate engages me in conversation. I find myself wondering if there is such a thing as death by bad breath. I have to cover my nose and mouth with a rag that some call a shirt. My cellie talks to me through the gap in his mouth where his teeth once were before they fell victim to methamphetamine. There is no escaping the putrid stench that spills from his mouth with every word he utters. I think to myself that he must have eaten a dirty diaper for breakfast. That thought makes me chuckle momentarily, but the levity fades quickly. I smile to keep from crying.

The conversation consists of him telling me that he is being transferred from USP Atwater in California because of a heroin debt to a Mexican gang that he could not pay. Rather than staying in Atwater, where he knew he would be stabbed or beaten to death for his failure to pay his bills, he checked into what is called, "Protective Custody." Convicts commonly refer to this as P.C. or "Punk City." Atwater is known for its violence and anger. Just a year before my cell-mate's voluntary transfer from the prison, a correctional officer was stabbed to death by two inmates. Maximum Security Prisons within the Federal Bureau of Prisons are places where neither staff nor inmates want to be. Sometimes people have to do things they do not want to do to feed their families. Sometimes people are packaged and shipped off to these prisons with no basis to object.

My time has come. I find myself thanking God for saving me from this cell-mate of mine. Three days in USP Atlanta's transfer hub is coming to an end. I think of the words etched into the wall.

"God save me."

I know my small prayer to get out of my concrete bunker with Diaper Breath John, or Mike, or whatever his name was, had been answered. I thank God that he is not on the same trip as me. Three days with him was almost unbearable.

It was 2:00 a.m. when I heard the knock on the door. I was taken to another cell filled with about sixty other screaming, excited convicts. They are all like me, dressed in rags, waiting to be packaged and then transferred to our new homes. Home Sweet Home! Convicted murderers mixed in with white collar criminals. Men with four-year sentences in cages with those who have life sentences. Lions with Zebras. Who cares? Just another day in the Federal Bureau of Prisons.

Around five in the morning we are separated, ushered into separate cells that resemble horse or cattle barns. Once in the stalls we are strip searched, our old rags are exchanged for paper-fabric jump suits, and foam smiley shoes. What better way to tell a prisoner that he's fucked than giving him foam shoes with a big smiley face on the front and have him walk across rocks. Maybe USP Big Sandy is not so bad after all.

Next is the packaging process. Shackles are put on and cannot be put on over socks. The cold metal bites into your skin and pinches your Achilles tendon. Each step is almost unbearable pain. I move to the next officer where my hands are cuffed in front of me. A menacing black box slides over my cuffs, then a waist chain is wrapped around me that the handcuffs are fastened to. The black box has cut off my circulation.

I notice only a few men with black boxes on their cuffs. The pain coupled with this observation prompts me to ask the officer why I have a black box.

"Officer, what's up with the black box? This shit's too tight!"

The officer snarls something unintelligible in his southern drawl. Tobacco juice spills over his brown stained lower lip.

"Why did you put this black box on me? The shit's too tight, man," I say as respectfully as I can under the circumstances.

"Shut the fuck up, and get on the bus, you dumb son-a-bitch." He leaves out the "of," as he degrades me. I smile sarcastically. I know deep inside that it is simply my circumstances that allows this officer to talk to me like this. In another life, if he ever talked to me like that, it would be the last time he did.

"You thinking somethin' funny son? "

"Not at all. Your house, your rules," I reply.

"Good. Follow them and get on the bus, you dumb son-a-bitch."

I find my seat. I ask myself if I can handle this ten-hour torture ride through the hills and the mountains. As the bus pulls out of the prison, the sun rises over this dark place. The small hills turn pink. Birds welcome the morning with sweet songs of happiness. The beautiful scenery outside the bus window is contaminated by my circumstances. The beautiful, red hills of Georgia that Dr. King spoke about look like shitholes from the dirty prison-bus windows. Slipping into an alternative mental state is the only place I might find some much-needed relief. Perhaps death would be more inviting. Maybe Death is waiting for me at United States Penitentiary Big Sandy. Who knows?

I must transform myself. I must become a beast in order to survive what awaits in this Federal Prison system. I am an alpha male, and I take this situation as a true challenge to the total mental breakdown. I imagine this whole thing will be a piece of cake. That thought is temporary. Two hours into this trip, and I realize how truly wrong I am. Dragging myself from this non-physical realm into a realm that seems like anything is possible is not easy. My vision must be clear, and not clouded by the non-truths that always seem to be bombarding the mind. Sitting in my seat, I begin to wonder how much pressure I can humanly take before it destroys the one thing that keeps my mind in check.

Up ahead is the doom that everyone dreads, wishing that it were not part of their lives. Mexicans are yelling profanity in Spanish and broken English. Another notch in the structure of my distorted mental being. My mental defenses kick in, and I find myself imagining butterflies— good times, fields of dreams. A naked woman before me—Monica

Mayhem, or some name like that. Porn star or not, for this brief moment she is all mine, mine alone. My mind pulls her close to me, and as our lips get ready to meet, my forefinger on her chin, my thoughts are interrupted. Ms. Mayhem disappears like a Chris Angel act. Fuck! I scream inside. I wish I could have her back.

"Hey amigo, what's happening?" A toothless Mexican in his fifties stares at me with a broken grin.

"I'm good, my man." I respond with anger in my voice, so he gets that I am not really looking for conversation.

I drag myself forward towards a destiny that no man should have to endure in twenty lifetimes, let alone one. For me, and the rest of us on this bus, we have no choice. Although some of us may have chosen the life we now have, some of us had no choice but to play the cards we were dealt. For many, the game was over before it ever began.

Onward we cruise. In time two Black inmates begin to taunt the Black correctional officers transporting us. My instincts, and earlier interactions with the out-of-shape White country ass correctional officer, tell me this cannot be good. In the back of the bus in his own cage, separated from the inmates, sits a big, Black officer with a shotgun locked, loaded, and ready for action. This job must have been option number two. At about 6'5 and 300 pounds or more, the NFL was likely hope number one; my guess is he came up short resulting in this gig. The fat White piece of shit with the tobacco stains on his lips is driving. He's got a pistol on his side. A lieutenant stands close by. He has another firearm.

Like lightning, the taunts echo off the metal core of the bus striking its victims, causing emotional damage that can only cause anger.

"Uncle Tom, let us get some music boss. We gonna be good, suh. So, you gets a good report with the White man. Yes, suh. We fo' sho is." One inmate yells this out in his best imitation of a Southern accent. The laughs from the other inmates only increase the anger on the Black lieutenant's face. Same with the big fella with the shotgun.

"Come on boss. You finna do us like that, suh?" The Southern chants slap their ears like a cymbal. Then comes the real voice, "Put the music on, house nigga." The Philadelphia accent is as clear as a new pipe drain.

The bus pulls off the highway into an old, abandoned McDonalds, and I have a feeling that while there will be no Happy Meals, there will be a few surprises. The two inmates from Philadelphia are ripped off the bus at gunpoint, the .12-gauge pointed at their heads. The shackles remain in place, the handcuffs come off, and now they meet my earlier fate. Black boxes are sunk tightly over the cuffs. The cuffs are tightened to the bones, the pain obvious on their faces. The men are shoved back on the bus. Everyone looks on in stunned silence.

The lieutenant huffs up the steps of the bus with Hill Billy Jim behind him. He pulls out a stun gun. Aiming it at the closest of the two, he says, "Keep yo shit up lil nigga, and I will zap your black ass. Now when you get to Sandy, have yo peoples call the White man and tell him I said that, Black ass nigga."

The bus is engulfed in silence. We work our way back to the highway, sailing closer to our destination of horrors. After a short time, the bus is alive again. The Mexican inmates start yelling back and forth to one another.

"What I would do for a box of tacos right now. Even from Taco Bell," the man next to me yells out, bringing phony hoots and hollers from the others. He leans in towards me, "You would hear nothing but wrappers Wado, and I don't mean the miatas."

The toothless Mexican chuckles. His chains shake on his belly.

I think he recognizes I have had enough when I say, "I wish I had them to give to you."

He smiles at me like a Jack-O-Lantern on Halloween night.

The yelling continues for what seems like an eternity; until we see the sinister dungeon in the distance. No one seems to know what to make of this distant, intimidating, ghoulish image coming closer to us. Many have heard the same rumors I have. I am not the only person who heard the reputation of this concrete jungle. Some have simply blown the rumors off as myth. Now their bowels quiver. The truth is staring them right in the face, unsettling stomachs. Too late to be scared now, but oh how I welcome the quietness that has overcome the population of this metal shuttle. Many of the macho images have now crumbled like the great walls of Jericho.

This is where my forty-year sentence will begin. It just might end here. The hands of death are rumored to be awaiting us behind these gloomy, grey walls. As we pull in, the wall opens, and it feels like the air has been sucked from my lungs. This was the moment that I prayed would never be my reality. Finally, it is.

The structure before us is a massive pile of slag with few windows. As the bus comes to rest my anxiety increases full throttle. Gasoline fumes dance lightly on the tip of my nose. The officers exit the bus to disarm. We are left on the bus for over thirty minutes while the officers' joke and make small talk with the Big Sandy staff. The waiting period seems like an eternity and I fidget with the chain and cuffs, out of boredom and nervousness.

A loudspeaker on the bus squawks, grabbing my attention.

"When you hear your name, come up here and give the Lieutenant your name and number, step off the bus and go through those doors right there. Oh, one more thing. Enjoy your stay here at Sandy. She's a good girl. If you treat her right, she'll be good to ya." Hillbilly Jim says this with a chuckle. I think he stole those last words from the Reba McEntire song, "Fancy."

The names are called out in alphabetical order, two at a time. "Johnson, Marks."

As luck would have it, Johnson is the Philadelphia convict who taunted the Lieutenant. I fall in behind him while he rattles off his name, then his prison number. The Lieutenant puts his hand on Johnson's chest and leans in, whispering loud enough for me to hear. "Now, you go ahead. Have *yo* peoples call the White man down in D.C. Snitchin' ass nigga." As Johnson steps off the last step, the lieutenant hollers towards the door, "They finna kill yo Black ass up here in these mountains."

I am staring into Hill Billy Jim's face. The man who earlier called me a son-a-bitch.

"Marks, 12010-055." I say this swiftly, hoping this is the last time I see him.

"Oh boy. Lieutenant, they finna kill this one right here too. He got a smart mouth like that dumb son-a-bitch Johnson." He smiles in my face. "Enjoy yo stay Mr. Marks. As long as it lasts."

Rather than respond I step down and off the bus. Gravel crunches under my foam smiley face shoes as I head into the doors and the truly unknown.

CHAPTER
TWO

INEZ, KENTUCKY WAS FIRST SETTLED by James Ward in 1810. Initially, Inez was named Armenta Wards Bottom. This community was made the seat of Martin County in 1873, replacing the earlier court at Warfield. Upon the occasion, J.M. Stepp renamed the area *Eden* after the Biblical garden. Stepp saw the place as beautifully decorated with trees, grass, and fresh, clean air. This is what God's *Eden* looked like to him. He like to think he never imagined his *Eden* would be contaminated by one of the most violent, brutal prisons ever known to man. Had he been able to see in the future, and the presence of Satan himself, he might have named the place *Humanity's Hell*.

Eden needed a new name. There was already a post office named *Eden*; the local postmaster was obliged to rename his Eden, Inez on June 23, 1874. The name Inez is usually held to have been derived from that of Inez Frank, the daughter of Louisa's postmaster in neighboring Lawrence County. Little did Inez Frank know back in the 1800s that her name would forever be intertwined with another name, "Sandy." That it would be coupled with felons, rape, robbery, violence, and even murder.

President Lyndon Johnson visited Inez, Kentucky, in 1964. While Inez's population of under one-thousand poverty-stricken inhabitants looked on, President Johnson landed a helicopter with his party at an abandoned miniature golf course to promote the War on Poverty. At that time, the poverty rate in this coal-mining area was greater than sixty percent. Many years after President Johnson landed in Inez, Kentucky, the city was gifted with a prison. With it came jobs.

Three-hundred and six acres of land were set aside to build this high security prison. The secure area that houses 1,253 inmates, on average, only compromises twenty-six acres of that land. An additional sixty-nine inmates are housed at the minimum-security camp, although that area is equipped to hold up to one hundred and twenty-eight convicted felons. Inmates housed at the camp provide the United States Prisons with a vital labor force.

Big Sandy sprawls over these three hundred and six acres, most of it rocky hillside. The main institution is secured by perimeter fences topped in razor wire, multiple, large, armed observation and gun towers, roving patrols, and electronic detection systems. Inside is a colony of desperate and, in most cases, lonely souls. Not just the prisoners. Staff too.

Prison is a two-sided world. It doesn't matter who you are—prisoner or staff—no one can walk through the doors of USP Big Sandy and leave unaffected. No one.

THREE

MY HEART RATE INCREASES but I try to remain calm. I'm projecting "Cool Hand Luke" himself. The neglected feeling increases though, with each biting step. I feel like the shackles are designed to bite into your ankles when you move. We are led to the R&D Department. A crowd of staff are milling around a long countertop and we are ushered into a small holding cell that smells like urine. All twenty-nine of us are jammed into a cell that would normally hold no more than ten men. The buzzing from the overhead, fluorescent lights vibrate my ear drums. The walls seem to be caving in on me. Claustrophobic or not, it is not a good feeling being cramped up with twenty-eight other men in a small cinder block bunker.

Before long, we are given clipboards, small pencils, and forms to fill out. It seems as if this is the last part of losing my life. Every time I sign my signature to a form, I feel like my John Hancock is another way of me saying goodbye to the real world. The last form gives permission to the staff to open and read all incoming mail. The last part informs me that any mail I send out cannot be sealed by me. It must be read, inspected, then sealed by a correctional officer.

The door of the holding cell is unlocked so the stench has an escape route.

"Marks 055," an officer calls out.

"Right here."

"Come with me."

I am back in one of the cattle stalls for the routine, all-inclusive, strip searches that come with leaving or entering a new prison. Once naked, I am ordered to bend over and spread my ass cheeks. Again, I find myself mad enough to pluck a chicken with my teeth. For me, there is nothing more humiliating then being strip searched by another man. The "spread 'em" part only intensifies the humiliation. The anger rises like bile in my throat. Anger is the one thing that I hold onto. Like many prisoners, it feels like the only thing that reminds me that I am still normal.

The intake process is long—fingerprinting, photos, medical evaluations, and a new monkey suit to tide us over until we make it to the laundry tomorrow. Elastic waist khaki pants, brown shirt, and orange slip-on shoes are issued to us. Once dressed, we are put back in our holding cell. Finally, the food arrives. I can feel my stomach touching my back. Brown paper bags containing one cheese sandwich, one bologna sandwich and a small container of warm milk. I have been eating bologna sandwiches for days now. I harbor some small hope that the food will get better.

Someone calls my name and number again. I am led to a small room for a security interview conducted by the Captain, Lieutenant, and a Special Investigation Services (SIS) officer. The captain speaks first.

"Take a seat Marks."

"Where you from, son?" The lieutenant belts out.

"First time in the feds I see," the captain says, and then lets out a loud whistle. "This cracker has a boat load of time. Forty fucking years." His eyebrows arch up as he looks over at the SIS Officer.

"What the fuck did you do?" the SIS officer asks with a surprised expression on his face.

"Crack cocaine case," is my only response.

"Did someone die?"

"Nah, man. They gave me five years for a .12-gauge hunting rifle, twenty-five years for a .22 rifle, and ten years for fifty grams of crack."

"That's that 924(c)-stacking shit, right?"

"Yeah, that's it."

"They have some dude from Utah all over the Internet for that shit. Wally or something…"

"Weldon Angelos?" I ask.

"Yah man, that's him. I read his story. They might change that shit. Then what would you have?"

"Fifteen years!"

"What happened on the bus?" asks the captain.

"Nothing."

"Well they told us you had a smart mouth. You're starting over here. Don't worry about it."

"Alright. I appreciate that."

"Well, you might not. But anyway, did you rat on anyone?'

"Nah, man"

"Never assisted law enforcement in any way? Rape kids?"

"Fuck no, man. What kind of question is that?"

"Mandatory questions, son. Now let's not get that mouth going. New start alright," the heavy-set lieutenant says as he coughs into his hand.

"Well you should make it here. At least for a little while," the captain chimes in with a small snicker. He clears his throat, "Well, conduct yourself like a man in here. Like a convict."

"Am I done here?"

"Possibly."

As I begin to rise, the captain tells me to sit back down.

"Look I don't know what you really did to get a forty-year sentence, but you seem semi-intelligent. This is a serious place. Do you understand that?"

"Actually, I do."

"Well, you don't come across like a typical convict. Do yourself a favor. Don't get no tattoos on your face. And get a knife because you're going to need one. That is the best advice I can give you."

"Thanks," I say, fully understanding that the meeting is over, but for some reason I cannot bring myself to my feet. All three men are staring at me. I wonder what they are really thinking. Have they seen other men this nervous? A nervousness that grips one's soul so deep that the body's mechanisms will not respond to the signals from the brain.

I shake it off. "Do you have anything else for me?"

"No. Send the next guy in."

My legs finally find themselves. I grip the hard-white, plastic chair arms. Rising to my feet, I find just enough courage to move forward. Forward to that destiny that no man should have to endure. My hand grabs for the door and as it swings open, I hear the three men behind me chuckle. Likely they have played this part over and over for many years before me, with similar men.

Twenty-eight men are still bottled up in the holding cell. As I make my way back there my heart races with fear and a sick sense of excitement. Thoughts are swirling through my mind like an Oklahoma tornado. Is this the Feds? The federal government? Did this guy just tell me to get a knife? For a minute I think I must have heard him wrong, that my mind is playing tricks on me, like that Ghetto Boys song. I replay the conversation over and over in my head hoping I am wrong. The sad truth is I have to get a knife because that's exactly what the captain said. My mind is not playing tricks on me, and it breaks another piece of my being inside. I cannot imagine what it would be like to be stabbed. The thought overwhelms me with fear. I guess it's a matter of stab or be stabbed.

All the stories I heard about Big Sandy are slowly beginning to manifest themselves. Why are they stabbing each other? How are they getting knives? I know in an instant that I don't want to be here for one minute without one. As the captain suggested, that's my first priority. I would rather be caught with a prison shank, than without one by some deranged felon bent on killing me for no apparent reason. The art of prison knife making is priority number one on my agenda list.

Prior to walking through the doors of doom, I would never have imagined a federal corrections officer, let alone a captain in a high position of authority, instructing me to get a knife. My insides shake with anxiety from my stomach to my brain. How I ever put myself in this position I will never truly understand. Prison will not be easy. Every day of my life behind these concrete walls will turn into a struggle just to survive. When I woke up in Youngstown, Ohio and looked into that mirror of despair, I told myself I was going to be alright no matter what happened. I no longer know if that is the truth.

My moment of solitude is interrupted when I hear a voice close to me say, "What did they say bro?" A bald-headed White guy covered in tattoos is talking to me.

"Nothing much! They said I was cool for the yard, told me to get a knife, then sent me back in here."

The White guy smiles, extending his hand, "They call me Shamrock bro. This shit is real over here. It's party time in Kentucky, bro."

I smile back sarcastically while I examine Shamrock, quickly assessing that he is a babbling idiot. I wish he would find someone else to talk to. I take issue with him calling me bro. I'm not his bro, or brother. The thought of pulverizing him here, now flirts with my conscience. It's been on my mind from the first hour of the bus ride. For a brief moment I fantasize about what his head would look like if my hand crashed into his jaw just to quiet him for the rest of the day. I stare at the tattoo across his neck. "SHAMROCK." It paints a clear target. If struck it would fold all one hundred and fifty pounds of him. In my mind I am querying whether if I hit him hard enough, one or more of his sixty or so tattoos would fall off.

Since the bus ride his mouth has been running like a well-oiled machine. His mission I guess was to make new guys think he was some tough prison gladiator, built for battle. I easily see through the facade and for a split second, I have empathy for him, knowing that this phony mask he is wearing is his own defense mechanism for what Big Sandy has in store for each of us. Shamrock is called out for his security interview, giving us a break from his counterfeit, prison war-stories.

Within minutes he is back, to our collective disappointment. I was secretly hoping he would vanish or be gone for at least twenty minutes.

"Damn!" he shouts. "The assholes are locking me up." He says it so everyone can hear him.

"How come?" I ask, curious.

"They got me down as a skinhead. Said my people don't walk here, so I got to go to the SHU."

With him having all the shamrocks tattooed on his body, he is supposed to be the lucky one, but for now luck has found me. My lips form a smile as things begin to register. I won't be seeing this asshole any longer. Finally, this annoying freak with the bro reference will no longer be a part of my life.

There is a knock on the window. The SIS Officer from earlier points at Shamrock, then curls his finger in a come here gesture. The door opens and the SIS officer tells a correctional officer to put Shamrock in a single cell by himself. As Shamrock walks out the door, the captain appears.

"Lock him up. Cell alone. Rec alone. He's PC-ing." Shamrock knows we all heard the captain. He walks towards the single cell with his head down. A defeated dog after a hard-fought battle.

Kelly, the guy who sat in front of me on the bus, slides close.

"That Shamrock, he's a punk. Checked in. Faking like he was a gangster. Man, he's soft," Kelly says with a grin.

"Why did he check in?"

"Man, I came with him from Terra Haute USP. One of his skinhead brothers got jumped on. He ran and didn't help the dude. That's why he can't walk here. He's got brothers on this yard. If he came out, they would kill him."

"Where is he from?"

"Wisconsin. I don't know about you, but I never met no tough guys from Wisconsin. Except the dudes who play for the Packers. Have you?"

"Nah, not really," I say. We both laugh loudly.

"That whole bus ride with his prison stories was a joke. He knows that once we hit the yard, I would have exposed his ass. Once a check-in, always a check-in. He's going to be in P.C. for the rest of his bid.

"For that shit at Terra Haute?"

"That, and there's some paperwork on him that he's a snitch. He did some legal work for someone and then wrote the dude's prosecutor. He can't go nowhere bro."

Kelly calling me bro does not anger me the way it did when Shamrock used the reference. Checking in is a mortal prison sin that is equivalent to snitching. Such a sin follows you from prison to prison. If caught, there is always some form of punishment to be paid for one's trespass. The penalty of such sin is atonement by one's own blood. The debt in prison can never be fully paid, but always collected when the opportunity presents itself. Shamrock is truly hit for the rest of his bid. Luck may never find him no matter how many shamrocks he has tattooed on his skin. Checking in means you tell staff you're not safe. That comes with telling on someone, or a group of people. Most times staff will not let someone check in unless they name someone. Such drastic actions come with severe consequences; consequences for people like Shamrock that will follow them for years to come.

The door swings open and a booming voice echoes off the walls.

"Alright men! Grab a mattress and a bedroll as you exit the cell. It's time to enter the House of Pain," a uniformed guard yells out.

Our names are yelled out along with a housing unit assignment and we are led out into a long hallway. The ground is hard concrete with a glistening shine. The long hallway is vacant except for us, the new inhabitants of this proclaimed House of Pain. The smell is distinctly clean. Everywhere is spotless. When we bend the corner, there is a larger metal detector and sliding jail bars that open and close both manually and electronically by whomever is manning the control booth. An old wall phone dangles upside down by its curly cord, a symbol of Big Sandy's defunct communication system.

As we walk on, I hear a screaming noise being emitted from a hand-held radio strapped to the lead officer's waist belt. My ears strain to hear. The sound of hard boots slaps the shiny concrete in rapid succession.

"All available units respond to the North yard immediately! Fight in progress. Possible weapons."

Oh shit, I think to myself. Officers are streaming past us, keys jangling on their belts.

"Get on the wall men!" the officer barks out. So, I find my way to the wall dropping my mattress, and bedroll in the process. The wall routine is to make a clear path so officers can respond to the many emergencies I am sure grip this prison like a death vise.

Within minutes a heavy-set White guy is raced down the hall on a stretcher. His face is a mutilated, bloody mess. I quickly understand that this is the party that Shamrock was talking about earlier. Within hours of my arrival, the party has already started. But it's simply not my kind of party.

For a fleeting moment I think to myself, I should have done what Shamrock did. At least I would be safe. Suppressing this thought comes easy, knowing if I did that I could never enter the general population here or at any other prison. One thing I can never do is, is check in. It would make for a rough forty years. After being against the wall, face first, for over ten minutes, we are pointed in the direction of the units we are to be housed in. Again, I feel like my legs do not want to move. Somehow, they do, and I march on to A-4 housing unit.

By the luck of the draw I am ordered to the same unit as Kelly. Three young, White convicts are walking towards us, handcuffed behind their backs with a six-officer escort. One of their eyes meets mine. He nods his head at me as if he recognizes me. I nod back as a sign of respect. My heavy mattress rests on my shoulder. These are the three men who recently wreaked havoc in the North yard on the man now in the prison infirmary. I would later learn that man's name is Skinner. His transgression was he tried to manipulate a nineteen-year-old White kid into performing oral sex on him. The nineteen-year-old went to the prison shot callers for help. Once he relayed the script, a hit on Skinner was sanctioned. In the White prison community, homosexual predators are not tolerated. Savage beatings are always inflicted as a form of deterrence.

"Look Chad, you're new to this shit," Kelly sighs. "So, this is what I'm going to do. I'm going to teach you the ropes bro. I've been down ten years. In some serious places. So, I know what the fuck goes on in here."

What the hell is it with this bro word and prison? I think to myself.

"I just came from Terra Haute with that lame Shamrock, and it was popping, bro. I know you're nervous. We all are, but you're going to be alright man. For real. Trust me." Kelly finishes with a smile and a handshake. He can recognize my nervousness.

"I hope so," I respond.

"Listen bro. Stick with your own in here, and don't fuck with niggers."

I look around instantly not believing what just came out of Kelly's mouth. The N-word! The majority of this place's population is Blacks. Seeing my reaction, he chuckles.

"Ah man, don't get bent out of shape over that. To them we're honkeys, crackers, white devils, and all kinds of shit. They call us what they want, we call them what we want. They know what they are."

Again, I am stunned by his words. Whispering I say, "Chill man, if they hear you talk like that, they'll kill both of us."

Kelly's eyes light up. "That's why we have to get some knives A.S.A.P. bro! Listen Chad, this is prison so I don't usually do this, but I'm going to treat you like a little brother, and basically teach you how things work in the feds, until you get the hang of this prison shit."

"That's cool with me," I answer with relief.

"Basic rules around here, man: First, stay away from drugs, selling, using, whatever. It always leads to problems. The same goes for gambling. Don't mess with no homos, stay away from gang dudes, and just to be politically correct for you, stay away from the African Americans. You're from New York, so don't start thinking you're an African American. That can get you in trouble in here." He laughs with his delivery. "You get in a gang in here, all you're looking for is a problem. Be your own man bro, and hopefully one of the honkeys in here will hit us off with a couple of knives."

"Man, I'm not trying to stab no one, for-real."

"Well I don't want to be in prison either, but guess what? I'm here and I'm trying to make it home. Ain't no one killing me in here. A knife is like an American Express card around here, bro. Never leave home without one."

"I guess it is what it is, right?"

As we get to the top of the stairs, I peer through the small window of the door. "You're going to be alright Chad. Trust me on this. And remember you're a honkey. Honkey's rumble, crackers crumble. What are you?"

"A honkey, I guess," I say with a smile, wondering where Kelly ever drummed up a saying like that. Maybe from his days growing up in Ohio. Who knows?

Again, I peer through the window in the door. The aperture is about five inches wide and thirty inches long. I see a stream of men yelling, playing cards, and others watching television. Hidden in my pants, my knees literally shake. I feel the bile well up, and a slight burning in my throat. Kelly slaps me on the back, jarring me back to reality. He reaches for a large, black button to the right of the door and a loud buzzing noise screeches out. Everyone inside looks towards the door. I step back from the window wondering what is in store for me inside.

Figure 1 - Sign - USP Big Sandy.

FOUR

U SP BIG SANDY did not just happen; it was years long work in progress. As our nation ran for the lead in being the strongest nation in the "Free World," it also ran to be the leader in incarcerating more of its citizens than any other industrialized nation in the world. The very sad reality is that "the land of the free," is actually less free than any other country on Earth. The United States is home to 5% of the world's population, but it is also home to 25% of its prisoners. The incarceration rate that plagues the United States is 19% higher than Turkmenistan's, 36% higher than the late Fidel Castro's Cuba, and 57% higher than Russia's. The United States has a higher prisoner count than most of the world's most notorious repressive regimes.

This system of mass incarceration costs the taxpayers, the government, and families of justice at least $182 billion per year. The costs associated with the system of mass incarceration include $80.7 billion for public corrections agencies including prisons, jails, and probation; $5.8 billion for prosecution; $63.2 billion for policing (only criminal law), and $12.3 billion for health care. Today, more than 2.2 million people are incarcerated in the United States. Between 1978 and 2009, the prison population in the United States rose by more than 425%.

With that rise, prisons like USP Big Sandy began to pop up in poor rural areas. With new prisons came much needed jobs for mostly poor White people, at the expense and anguish of poor Black and Hispanic communities. Today, one out of every ten African Americans is in prison.

Every American state has its prisons, as do most countries. Most people simply accept imprisonment or incarceration as the normal penalty for those who commit more serious crimes. In today's world, we tend to associate prison with hard discipline, or punishment. It was not always that way. At their beginning, prisons were promoted as strongholds of the Enlightenment. These prisons were looked upon not only as a means to rehabilitate the criminally wicked, but to ultimately cleanse society of crime altogether. It was believed that the cleansing process—imprisonment—would make orderly societies safe for democracy. Initially, these prisons were called "Penitentiaries," as Big Sandy is today. This was because they promised to induce holy penitence in their prisoners. That promise is far from the truth within penitentiaries across the United States nowadays.

The rise of the penitentiary is tied with the rise of American democracy. Prisons are not new; they are in fact as old as civilization itself. However, until modern times, they were seldom used to confine criminals for lengthy periods, much less for rehabilitation.

In the new world, the rule of law usually relied on a much cheaper form of punishment—pain and shame. The tools of justice were branding, stocks, and the most feared: lashing with whips. The objective, according to the people ordained to administer justice, was not to cure crime, which was impossible, but to control it to some extent. To check man's inclination toward sin. The social hierarchy was enforced by a range of penalties. Free and propertied Whites could circumvent even the most serious convictions with a fine. Outsiders generally faced expulsion. White servants, Indians, slaves, and free Blacks were most often punished by the lash.

The gallows were always there in the background. The ultimate penalty for serious offenders and repeat offenders of all kinds. These terrible public punishments made for a great show, but local governments found it hard to control their communities' interpretations. And colonial cities were growing. Gruesome penalties discouraged juries from delivering guilty verdicts, with more crime a predictable aftereffect. Prominent Americans called for change. They felt bloodthirsty punishments were unfit for the budding, emergent Age of the Market; that the gallows were simply too harsh an instrument of discipline; and that lashing—whip rending actual flesh— was overly severe.

Americans leaving the mother country devoted time to ending the "bloody code" of the old country. Kings considered their people their property, so shedding their blood came as easy as slaughtering one of their calves. Although the people of the new land pushed back against sanguinary sanctions, they also understood that there must be some punishment for one's transgressions. In a democratic society, the great land of liberty, man had to be held responsible for his actions; man could not be permitted to do as he pleased. Thus, came the proposal for a "Penitentiary."

A medical doctor, and a signer of the Declaration of Independence, Benjamin Rush, proposed that "a large house be erected" capable of "reforming criminals and preventing crimes." Big Sandy was being molded from the beginning of the United States absent the reforming criminals and preventing crimes. Could Big Sandy and my forty-year sentence ever reform me? As for a place that prevents crime? Violent crime is rampant in this concrete doom castle.

Figure 2 - USP Big Sandy.

CHAPTER

FIVE

EAR AND ANXIETY RIP THROUGH ME like hurricane Katrina. Knowing I cannot let these feelings destroy me, I gather my composure. A large metal key, a sound that I have become accustomed to, clangs against a dirty door with what appears to be faded blood spatter across the bottom. I see a guard with small, brown beady eyes and a baseball cap peering through the small window at me and Kelly.

"New guys?" he muffles through the door.

"Yah," Kelly yells back. To myself I think, *No asshole, we been in your unit for years. Of course, we're new guys.* The guard has a sarcastic smile on his face as he turns the key.

"Well bro, here it all is," Kelly says. My mind regurgitates the words I heard earlier. "All I can tell you young man, is get a knife." Stab or be stabbed vibrates from my forehead to the back of my head.

I grip my mattress tightly as the door swings open. All eyes focus on us—the two new White guys. The din produced by a hundred or more men envelopes me, swirling through my ears like a windy day. Cigarette smoke dances in my nostrils although tobacco products are prohibited in the federal prison system. Fluorescent lights pierce my eyes. It takes a moment for my eyes to adjust. Everything seems to be moving in slow motion. The guard rattles off our cell assignments. A group of White convicts approaches. The first guy extends his hand.

"They call me Lefty," he says as we shake hands.

"Chad," I respond. I notice Lefty has no right arm. Clearly, his name, Lefty, stems from his missing arm. I want to laugh, but I suppress the urge.

"What cell is he going in C.O.?" Lefty inquires.

"107."

"Oh, hold on C.O. Chad, check this out bro, the cell they're trying to put you in, the kid who lives in there thinks he's Black. He runs with the Blacks. You're with the Whites, right?" Lefty's question is in earnest.

"Yea, man. Most definitely," I respond, remembering Kelly's Prison 101 speech. Lefty darts off in the direction of the guard. My ears focus in on his conversation.

"This kid ain't going in that cell. We have some open White cells and we'll find a place for him and let you know where he's going to be living in a minute."

"Well, when you get it all figured out let me know. I'll be in the office Lefty." The guard with the beady eyes and dirty baseball cap heads towards the office.

I stand there in awe. I am not showing it on my face though. Things slowly sink in. Lefty just told the guard what was going to happen, and the guard had no objection. It is surprising to me that a prisoner can tell a guard what was going to transpire, and that the guard accepted it. It is easy to see that the convicts are calling the shots in this prison. I know full well that such circumstances cannot be good.

A group of White convicts surrounds me, pelting me with questions. It reminds me of when I was a small child with a new puppy. It was exciting, something new. For these men, a new inmate is exciting because he brings stories from the streets, stories from other prisons, he brings change to days that always seem the same. Most people have different experiences every day. Prisoners have the same experience every day, for years—some forever.

The questions come from all directions.

"What's your name, bro?"

"Where are you from?"

"How much time you got, bro?"

I answer each question in quick succession. "My name is Chad. I'm from New York. I got forty years on a crack case." The forty-year answer triggers a whistle from a fat, White guy they call K.Y., Lefty's cell mate.

"Damn! They ain't playing no games on that crack shit," he says in a Kentucky drawl.

Everyone in the group shakes my hand and introduces themselves. Two of the men share the fact that they are serving life sentences. One for murder, the other for a methamphetamine case out of the great state of Texas. The Texas cowboy tells me in his words that he was a "junkie," just delivering meth so that he could get high. He was pulled over, and because of two prior drug possession charges for small amounts, his new conviction mandated a life sentence. It seems like these guys are embracing me. Perhaps this thing won't be so bad after all.

If I really believed that notion, I would only be tricking myself.

"Chad, come here for a minute."

Lefty calls me to his cell. I stand at the door. When he senses my reluctance to enter the cell, Lefty begins to laugh. "Come in man. You watched too many fucking prison movies. You're cool man."

I laugh with him. "Yah man, you're probably right," I say as I walk into the cell.

"Check this out Chad. We got to find you a house to live in. You can go in with this kid Eric, or with this old man, Mr. Young we call him."

"Well, who do you think is better?"

"I don't know bro. They both have negatives. The kid, Eric, is a retard who almost stirred up a race riot in here. Mr. Young, he's an older guy stuck in his own ways. He goes to bed early, up at five o'clock every morning. It's like living with your old ass grandfather," Lefty tells me.

Hearing the race riot thing helps me make a quick decision, and I tell Lefty that Mr. Young sounds like a much better choice for me. He agrees. I watch him walk towards an old man with white hair. Another guy walks up to me and introduces himself.

"Hey kid, I'm Louie from Boston. How are ya doing? Ya like this place yet? It's a shit hole."

I haven't been here long enough to really answer Louie, so my response is a simple, "We'll see, huh."

Lefty is waving me over. "Chad, this is Mr. Young."

I reach my hand out. Mr. Young begins to interrogate me. The first question is whether or not I snore. I tell him I don't.

He says, "Well that's good cause if you did, you'd have to go in there with ole trouble making Eric." His next question is whether or not I go to bed early. He explains that he cannot have a cellmate that wants to stay up all night. After a few more questions he finds me suitable. I can live with him.

Mr. Young walks me over to the cell I will be sharing with him, as if he does not want some new intruder in there alone. Finally, I am able to put my heavy mattress into a bunk and I can at least hope for some much-needed rest this evening. My first thoughts are that Mr. Young is very clean. I do a once over on the cell. It is immaculate. The floor is freshly shined, and it appears to have a new coat of wax. A few makeshift throw rugs cover parts of the floor. Several home-made cardboard shelves are affixed to the walls. A large Country Cottage calendar hangs on one wall. If there is such a thing as a homely feeling in prison, this cell is such a thing.

The Country Cottage calendar is not something I expected to see in Big Sandy. For a brief moment it makes me think of my grandmother. I faintly remember her house being decorated with Country Cottage paraphernalia and knick-knacks. Even these brief thoughts of home, and good times, hurt so when they show up I try hard to push them away.

My thoughts are interrupted. Mr. Young offers me some soap, a razor, and shampoo. He points at a pair of shower shoes on the floor, and tells me I can use them when I shower.

"If you don't use 'em you'll have athletes' foot, and I don't want no one in here with their feets itchen." He says this in a southern drawl. I thank Mr. Young for his generosity. I am in need of a shower. As I slip off my prison shoes, Mr. Young interrupts me.

"Oh, no son. You gotta wear them sneakers to the shower. Put the shower shoes on in the shower. When you get out, dry your feet and put your sneakers back on."

"Does everyone do that?" I ask.

"Yah. Anything can happen around here, and you'll see that soon. You don't want to be slipping and sliding around here if something happens." I nod in agreement and slide my sneakers back on. Lefty is right behind me as I head to the shower.

"Hey Chad, I'm going to stand point for ya man." Lefty says.

"What?"

"Look man, anything can happen here at the drop of a hat. Being in the shower, naked, is a vulnerable position. So, what we do is when we shower, we take a White dude with us to stand outside the shower. We get each other's backs around here. We always keep a knife on us."

"Man, this prison shit is crazy." I reply, thinking about the knife thing again.

"Crazy, and dangerous, bro. Go ahead, shower. I got you."

After the shower I make the rounds. Lefty chaperones me around the housing unit and I meet new convicts. I learn how things are run here at USP Big Sandy. There are many rules, and convict codes. The things that register quickly are the consequences. I am told that for certain violations, you could be stabbed, hit in the head with a padlock attached to a belt, or with a pipe. The violations that attract these types of punishments include snitching, selling knives, or weapons, to other races, and masturbating in the open in front of female staff members. These are called "yard violations." Yard violations invite swift consequences. My brain registers each of them swiftly and I commit to never violating any of the yard rules.

Lefty introduces me to Nick who gives me the rundown on how this place operates. Nick is twenty-five years old and serving a thirteen-year sentence for crack cocaine conspiracy in Buffalo, New York. Given Nick is from Buffalo, and in my age bracket, I click with him instantly. Being we are from the same area we are what they call "home boys" in prison. Nick offers me some food and a soda.

My response is what I learned from prison movies. "Man, I'm cool, but thanks anyway." I say this despite that my stomach is rumbling from hunger, and too many bologna sandwiches that I could not choke down.

Nick laughs at me. "Listen Chad, I know you're hungry after that trip. Screw all them prison stories dog. Eat. You don't owe me nothing. We're home boys man."

I laugh and look back. I think about how Nick obviously took the same trip I took, and when he got here he was likely as hungry as I am. After his speech, with my stomach rumbling, and the smell of the burritos I eagerly accept the food. Me and Nick hang out in the day room and talk for a while. I notice some of the White guys looking at us funny. I mention it to Nick. He tells me the Whites do not like him because he is in the Black, New York car. I don't ask what a car is, but I think back to just a few hours ago. Lefty intervened when I was assigned to a cell with another White guy who Lefty said, "thinks he's Black." I wonder if it was Nick.

Almost on cue I hear a Correctional Officer yell, "Alright men. Let's go. Night's over! Lock it up! Lock it in."

There is no time to ask Nick questions, and I am kind of relieved. I shake his hand and I head over to my new cell. I suspect there will be no cockroaches, or mice scurrying for cover when the lights come on in the morning.

Every night at 9:45 p.m. we are locked in our cells until 5:30 a.m. As I climb into my bed, I think about how my first day in a real federal prison has come to a close. My eyes are heavy, and I imagine the lights will be going out as soon as the door is locked. Mr. Young decides to break his number one rule by not going to sleep early. He engages me in conversation.

Mr. Young tells me that he is sixty-three years old, and that Big

Sandy has been his home for the last four years.

"You know Chad," he says, in my sixty-three years of life, I ain't never seen the violence that I have seen in this prison. You been anywhere with vicious violence?"

"Not really. Not no prison at least."

"About a month ago there was two guys beating another fella with a padlock on a belt outside. The officer in the gun tower fired a shot and hit the guy that was getting beat."

"What?" This wakes me up. "How the hell they shoot the guy getting beat?" I ask with stunned curiosity.

"Well, they ain't that smart round here. That's why I ain't been to the yard since. Don't want one of 'em to shoot me on accident."

Mr. Young keeps on rolling. My eyes grow heavier, begging for rest. He fills me in on another assault that happened in the Unit I am assigned to, A-4, just a few months prior. From what Mr. Young tells me, there was a guy who lived in this unit that was part of a gang called, "The Dirty White Boys." This gang has a lot of problems with other White prison gangs, and there was a plot to rid Big Sandy of any Dirty White Boy gang members.

The morning had begun like any other, but before long four White inmates came into the unit looking for the lone Dirty White Boy. Once he was spotted a guy from Kentucky who called himself "Seven," grabbed the Dirty White Boy in a bear hug from behind, while two others helped Seven wrestle the guy to the ground. Once on the ground another guy, Jerry Lee, stabbed the Dirty White Boy numerous times, and once in the eye. The Dirty White Boy was life flighted out of the prison. Medical staff saved his life, but they were unable to repair his eye. The eye had fallen victim in *Humanity's Hell*—USP Big Sandy.

Mr. Young's stories do not stop. He tells me about a race riot that broke out between Black and White inmates. The White inmates were outnumbered and came out on the bad end of the gruesome assault. Correctional Officers stormed the unit firing high-powered bean-bag guns that left deep dents in the steel doors.

As I am beginning to drift off to sleep my thoughts are that Mr. Young is a walking USP Big Sandy newspaper. In the old days he might have been called the Town Crier. After the long bus ride, I am utterly exhausted. Briefly I wonder if going into Eric's cell with his stories about Adolf Hitler might have been better. Mr. Young was still going when sleep finally found me. The last thing I remember is fear rippling through my veins like cold ice water. Surviving this barbaric dungeon seems impossible. In my dream, I am falling into a deep, dark abyss. I am screaming, but nothing comes out and then I wake up sweating, longing for water. My hands go to my eyes to make sure they are still there. The fear prevents me from falling asleep again.

Mr. Young's alarm is beeping. He pulls himself up from his bunk. The doors unlock at 5:30. No one sleeps in around here for fear of someone coming into your cell and taking your eyes out while you're in dream land. The unwritten rule is that no one sleeps unless the doors are locked. Those who do run the risk of death, or a vicious assault.

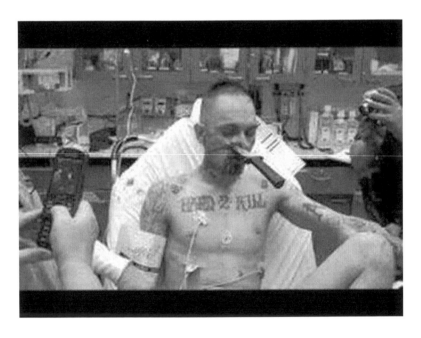

Figure 3 – Result of prisoner being stabbed with homemade shank.

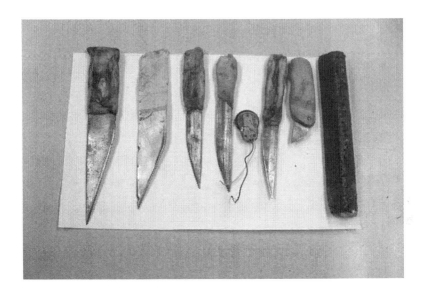

Figure 4 - Sampling of confiscated prison shanks.

SIX

KELLY MEETS ME IN THE DAY ROOM. My eyes adjust to the lights as Kelly reaches his hand out.

"How'd ya sleep man?"

"Not bad," I lie. My night had not been good. How could it have been after all of Mr. Young's stories? The morning has just begun, and I am already dreading what stories my cellmate will tell me once we are locked in tonight.

"You hungry Chad?"

"Starving," I respond.

"They should be calling chow any minute bro."

A correctional officer unlocks the door to the unit and calls Chow. I follow behind Kelly and we make our way to the mess hall. The hallway is crowded with what looks like a herd of inmates. People are yelling back and forth as they hurry to breakfast.

As we approach the mess hall, Kelly says, "Just follow me."

There are two doors, with two serving lines. We fall into the line that the White, and Hispanic inmates form. Black inmates form their own line on the other side.

All eyes—at least those belonging to the other White inmates—are on us. We pick up empty food trays and slide them on a counter. Different inmates put different food items on each tray. First scrambled eggs, then oatmeal, two biscuits and a heaping scoop of gravy. After eating slop in county jails, and in Youngstown Ohio, I am a little excited about the food on my tray. The White inmates sit in their own area of the mess hall, as do the Black, and Hispanic, inmates. Both Kelly and I make our way to the White section.

An inmate with a fully tattooed face asks, "Who you ride with?"

Kelly takes control. In an aggressive voice he says, "We're independents. Where do we sit?"

Tattooed face points to a table at the end of the line.

As we sit down, Kelly whispers, "Man, I hate those gang dudes bro. They think they are tough. They ain't shit for real." I ask Kelly what the hell this car thing means. He explains a car is a group of people that stick together for good, and bad. After a long explanation, I conclude a car is nothing but a gang with a more polite name. For example, a car might be a group of inmates from New York. Their leader is someone everyone looks up to. He has the keys. In other words, he's the driver. The Whites have a bunch of different sects. Some are white supremacist gangs, some are White guys with no gang affiliation, but there is one supreme leader who has the keys for the yard for all the White inmates. The same goes for the Black, and Hispanic, inmates.

In prison politic hierarchy, I am labeled a White Independent. I don't belong to a gang, or group. For the most part, I am at the low end of the totem pole around here, and on my own. Being on your own in prison is not the best choice. When you are by yourself in prison, it is like being a lone zebra near a pride of hungry lions on the African plains. Even on day one it's easy to see that as a zebra in here you can easily find yourself in a bad situation. Plus, vultures are lurking all over the place.

Once breakfast is over, we head to the prison laundry for our government issued clothing. The process takes hours. We stand in a line in the hallway. This is nothing like clothes shopping at the local mall, but this is still America. There will be commerce. As I wait in line various inmate vendors attempt to sell me a variety of products—sneakers, Walkman radios, and cigarettes. One guy offers to sell me heroin. I decline the offers. Laundry issues me two pairs of khaki pants, two shirts, brown boxer shorts, t-shirts, socks, a Velcro belt, and a pair of new boots, heavy as cinderblocks.

After the laundry process, we head to the medical department where a variety of tests are done on me. More questions are asked and answered. Shortly after the medical process is finished, I make my way to the commissary. I buy my own sneakers, some personal clothing, hygiene products, and some food.

Big Sandy is like a small town. There's an infirmary as the hospital, a commissary instead of a department store, chapel for a church, exercise yard as a park, gym as a health club, mess hall as a restaurant, correctional officers as their own little police department, and even a jail inside the prison. This jail is called the Special Housing Unit, but there is nothing special about that place.

The afternoon will bring a new aspect to my life in this small town. There is no way to avoid the recreation yard. I am told some of my other "home boys" want to meet me. Once lunch is over, inmates are permitted to go to the yard. This is not an adventure that I look forward to, but one I must embark on.

Figure 5 - USP Big Sandy prison yard.

CHAPTER
SEVEN

ONCE AGAIN, THE HALLWAYS ARE ALIVE. Inmates off to work, the education department, chapel, and the yard. I find myself walking through a metal detector that is unplugged. The machine is here to serve a purpose—prevent prisoners from going to the yard with knives, or weapons. It quickly becomes clear that the metal detectors are no more than decoration—ornaments dangling from a Christmas tree. There is no correctional officer present to man the machine even if it were plugged in. The only purpose these things seem to serve is that when important people show up for an inspection, they look good.

When I step out of the building the sun hits my skin for the first time in a long time. My skin glistens and I inhale the fresh mountain air. The air teeters on the edge of my nose and tickles my lungs. The warm sun and the fresh air feel good and trigger my thoughts. My last day as a free man bangs about in my subconscious mind. I think of it as if it were just yesterday, although it has been years. This is the closest I have been to freedom in five years. The thoughts sting, awakening a pain deep inside my heart.

The county jails that I have been living in have no outside yard. There was no sun to see, or fresh air to breathe, nor any wind to feel. I begin to reflect on my life as I walk through the gauntlet of fences, gun towers, and razor wire. *What has my life become?* I ask myself as I scan the yard.

The yard is not one big yard. Rather, it is one big field separated into four areas. Each section is separated by fences, gates, and locks. The tops of the fences are adorned with spirals of gleaming razor ribbon. The main yard has a quarter mile track with a makeshift football field that also doubles as a soccer field in the middle. Benches, and tables are scattered around the yard. They all belong to different groups, gangs, and cars. This makes finding a place to sit down and enjoy the weather difficult.

I survey the rest of the yard. There is a small portion where two walls sit on a concrete slab. This is where the inmates play handball. Further down is a volleyball court sitting in its own sand pit. To the right are two horseshoe pits. There is another large area that contains a neatly tailored baseball diamond. I feel the wind again as it whips across the fresh cut grass, the sun dazzling off the blades. Now I know why Kentucky is called the blue grass state. A bluish tint dances on the grass as my mind takes me back home. While I gaze at the diamond I am back in middle school playing second base, waiting for the batter to swing at the ball. I snap myself back to my reality. This is not the place for daydreams.

The last yard is behind me. It is made up of basketball courts, tables on the sides. I focus on one area of tables. There is a table with a white sheet tied on top of it; it flaps slightly in the breeze. A precision blackjack replica has been drawn on the sheet. The other sheets are similarly decked out—hand drawn carbon copies of poker tables. This looks like they were stripped off a Las Vegas gambling table at Mandalay Bay, but in reality, they are simply prison-made gambling paraphernalia.

My moment of peace was broken by a Black inmate who introduces himself as "Hustle Man." He has a display, different items for sale. There are sneakers, boots, clothes, magazines, artwork, homemade cards that look better than Hallmark, and food items. The crown of this little flea market stand is the sneakers. He's strategically placed one sneaker on top of the boxes with the other inside.

"You new here ain't ya?" Hustle Man asks.

"Just got here yesterday."

"Where you from?"

"New York. Upstate Rochester."

"Oh yeah? I'm from Brooklyn, and there are a bunch of homies from New York on this yard. Might be two, or three from Rochester. You running with the White boys though?"

"Yah man. You know how that goes."

"Shit. That don't mean you can't spend no money with the Hustle Man though. I got everything for sale. What you need man?"

"I'm good. I just went to commissary."

"Hold up, Rochester. I got something the commissary ain't got. I got da ladies my friend."

He rifles through a bag and pulls out a stack of over two hundred photos. He hands me the stack of photos. I shuffle through them, all attractive women. Some are naked, others have very little clothing on. "I told you Rochester. I got what the commissary ain't have." He says this with a sly smile. His entrepreneurship skills are on full display. I am reminded of the hustlers in Manhattan with three card molly, and the ball and cup game. This guy strikes me as the guy that runs hustles in New York City when he's not in prison.

Hustle Man has me with the photos. It has been a long time since I've seen a naked woman, even if she's only in a photo.

"How much for the photos?" I ask.

"Naked ladies go for eight stamps. The other sexy things go for four. I got a deal for you cause you're from Rochester. Two naked, two sexy—one book." I look at Hustle Man as if he is speaking a language I do not know, and he senses this.

"Ain't no one told you how da money work round here huh?"

"Nah, not really man."

"Boy, you green as a mutha fucka ain't ya? Look here. Money around here is stamps. Postage stamps. Every stamp equals twenty-five cents." At this he pulls some stamps out of his pocket to show me. Some of them are very old, others look new. "You got to have spending money on ya Rochester. You wasn't running around broke out there was ya?"

"Nah I wasn't broke."

"Okay, how much time you got?"

"Forty years."

"Holy shit was you killing people, or making money?" He laughs.

I respond with the usual. "Crack Case."

"Man, them White folks ain't playin' up there in Rochester. Anyway, with that kind of time you gonna have to find you a hustle. It takes money to make money."

I hand Hustle Man back his stack of photos and tell him I will get back to him when I get some stamps.

Hustle Man hollers at me when I am about ten feet away. "Rochester, don't be coming back window shopping my ladies wit out no money in your pocket. I don't play about my ladies." He says this with a chuckle as I try to distance myself from him.

I can't help but laugh to myself as I walk around the track. I haven't seen any violence yet. And this place reminds me of a flea market. People are selling all kinds of things: tootsie pops, sodas, deep fried burritos that they call Chimichangas. The Changas are stuffed with meat, cheese, onions, peppers, and ramen noodles.

Fresh mountain air fills my lungs, and the sun beats on my face. Things that I, like so many, took for granted, are now forever precious. In and out, out and in. I find myself satisfying my lungs with gulps of the fresh air. Prison makes me realize how valuable freedom truly is. The sun seems contaminated by the characters I see in the yard. Some of these men look like they walked straight out of a horror flick. Many of the White inmates are covered in tattoos, some of them have their faces painted with ink. It is hard to understand why anyone would do this to their face, and now I understand what the lieutenant meant when he told me not to get tattoos on my face. His advice was appreciated, but not needed. Never in ten lifetimes would I do such a thing.

A White inmate introduces himself to me as Half Dead. The shock on my face must have been evident.

"The name Half Dead is cause I'm half dead. Life sentence bro." Half Dead comes across as a guy who fears no one, and nothing. There is a tattoo across his forehead that reads, "White Pride." The rest of his head, neck, and body are tattooed in Neo-Nazi sayings. A portrait of Adolf Hitler covers his right side, along with the numbers 14 and 88.

I ask Half Dead, "What's the 14 mean?"

"It stands for the fourteen most important words to the White race," he tells me. "We must secure the existence of our race, and a future for White children,'" he says.

"How about the 88?" I ask, curious.

"The 88 stands for eighty-eight precepts, or ideas for conscious living of the White man."

My first thought is Half Dead would have fit in many years ago with the Nazi party back in Germany in 1933. He likely would have been a good SS Soldier under Heinrich Himmler, or some other crazed Nazi. My second thought is this is one of the guys Kelly warned me to stay away from.

The numbers 14 and 88 are products of a man named David Lang. Half Dead decides to give me a White history lesson. I listen out of curiosity. I gather from his lecture that Mr. Lang's objective in life was to rob enough armored trucks and banks to fund the purchasing of a substantial amount of land in the North Western United States. Once the land was purchased, he planned on it becoming a new homeland for the White race. Lang had Adolf Hitler in Nazi, Germany ambitions. In the end though, he only succeeded in becoming a federal prisoner and dying in a cell. From what I gather, David Lang has a lot of influence with the White prison gang members. Most of them have a 14 and an 88 tattooed on their bodies.

More White inmates are now flocking to the yard, and as the new White guy, everyone wants to meet you. A skinny White guy with long hair walks up to me and Half Dead. The man tells me his name is Dinky, and that he is the shot caller, or leader, for the Aryan Brotherhood of Texas gang. It is hard for me to imagine this guy as anyone's leader. He looks like a drug addict to me. I keep my thoughts to myself as he asks me questions. He wants to know if any ABT gang members came with me. I tell him, I'm not sure.

Our conversation is interrupted when a Black inmate starts screaming at the top of his lungs while he runs in a circle on the football field. My eyebrows arch up as I zero in on him.

"You know who I am. Soldier Boy! Any of you fuckers want to get down, let's go! I'll do it to yo mamma, and your heroin ass daddy."

"What the hell is the matter with that dude?" I ask bewildered. Both Dinky and Half Dead start laughing.

Dinky says, "That dude is a bug out."

"A what?"

"He's a bugout—a mental health patient," Half Dead interrupts. "We call him Soldier Boy. Dude does that shit all day long, bro. Everyday, screaming crazy shit."

I see Soldier Boy hitting himself in the head with the palm of his hand. "Is he really crazy?" I ask.

"Yea, something ain't right with that nigger," Dinky says, shaking his head. Half Dead laughs again. It's apparent to me, after only a few minutes of observing Soldier Boy, that he is mentally ill.

It does not take long after that for me to realize that a large portion of inmates are mentally ill. The county jails were flooded with them. Some of their symptoms range from the fairly mild—talking to oneself, failing to bathe—to more severe—men who don't know who they are, or where they're at, some who light their own cells on fire, men that are so hurt that they slash their wrists or attempt to hang themselves from cell bars, and fixtures.

Stress has a way of worsening almost any condition, and prison is incredibly stressful. Many men have broken down for the first time in their lives when they reach prison. Not only does prison make mentally ill people worse, it also has a way of driving people crazy. In Big Sandy, I am sure I will encounter many more men on the brink of being crazy, and others like Soldier Boy who is already there.

The homeboys who sent me the message to come outside never show up. I say my good-byes to Dinky and Half Dead and I work my way back to the housing unit. It is nearing four o'clock. Each day at four we are locked back into our cells for a head count to make sure we are not only still confined in this concrete jungle, but still alive. Once back in the unit, Mr. Young tells me that my homeboys said to come outside after dinner. They'd been sidetracked earlier in the day.

My afternoon in the yard flew by. The small sense of freedom penetrated my inner soul like a hunter's sharp arrow piercing a deer in the wild. For the first time in many years, I was able to walk around unchained. Here there are no cuffs on my hands, no shackles biting into my ankles. The feeling of being a chained dog has dissipated to some degree. I rejoice in this new feeling, but the pain still remains. As I look around the cell, I realize this is my new life. The reality of prison hits me like a ton of bricks. This new life reserved behind concrete walls is steel, anger, violence, and most of all—loneliness.

Before long I find myself back on the yard. The atmosphere has changed dramatically since this afternoon. Hundreds of men of all ages and races are milling around the yard. My instincts and my senses are heightened. The possibilities of bad things happening out here are evident. Instantly I can feel tension. The fresh air that I enjoyed earlier is now contaminated by a pressure that seems to be lurking on the horizon.

In the distance I see a man about 6'1", 250 pounds with long black hair beelining in my direction. Within seconds he is upon me. As his outstretched hand meets my own, he introduces himself, "Adam. You must be Chad?"

"Yah, Chad. How are you?"

"Good," he responds. "You need anything?"

"No, man. I am all set."

"Well, we knew a White dude from New York was coming. We saw your name on the bus list with a 055 number, so we were waiting on you," Adam says as he clears his throat.

"Yah well some people told me you wanted to meet me. They kind of gave me the run down on this place." I say.

"Is this your first spot?" Adam asks.

"Yah, first federal prison."

"Do you know about paperwork? Did anyone tell you about that?"

"Just a little bit in the county jail. I kind of heard you got to get your transcripts or something?" I say.

"Well, what we do is give you thirty days to get your docket sheet, sentencing transcript, and judgment of commitment. Just to make sure you're not a Cho-Mo."

"A what?" I respond.

"A Cho-Mo man. Child molester, or a rat, or snitch. That type of shit."

"Nah man, I'm no Cho-Mo. And I went to trial and got forty years."

"Yah, we had one of the cops check you out already, but that's just general info on their computers. We just need you to get that paperwork. It's your driver's license around here." Adam goes on.

"I'll write my lawyer, or the court, and get it for you." I say.

"Come on. Let's spin the yard so I can introduce you to some of the fellas from New York, and Boston." Adam says, and we head to the track.

The track is similar to the one from my high school days. While we walk, I notice the sun bouncing off the asphalt making it look like small diamonds are embedded and glistening there. Adam is waving to a group of four or five guys, summoning them.

One of the guys that Adam introduces me to is stone cold drunk. He reeks of booze. Being drunk in here has to be like a freight train on a collision course. As I reach out to shake the drunkard's hand, I hear a guy behind us tell Adam that the Sureños are going to hit one of their guys.

"They hitting Creeper," he says, and he nods towards the bathroom.

My gaze goes from the drunkard to the bathroom area where I can see a bunch of Hispanics milling around one man who I suppose is Creeper.

We all focus our attention on the bathroom area. We see the first punch—a sucker punch—meet its target. It comes from a man about 6'1" who towers over his prey by at least a foot. The victim stumbles back and his long black hair tumbles in waves from the impact. Creeper begins to swing wildly but two more inmates pounce on him like wolves on a small buffalo. Within seconds, Creeper falls to the ground like a limp log felled at the hand of a chainsaw operator.

I am stunned looking on. Two more Mexican inmates move in and they commence to stabbing their mark with homemade plastic knives. A siren blares over our heads when the first gunshot rings out, startling me. The shotgun blast—a warning shot—echoes through my ears like thunder pounding the side of a mountain in a desolate storm. Creeper seems to be unconscious, but the assault continues. The onslaught of violence reminds me of seeing two pit bulls attacking a person on the TV show, *When Animals Attack.* These men too, are animals.

Another gunshot rings out, followed by a concussion grenade fired from the gun tower that is only feet away from the melee. There is mass confusion now. Prisoners are attempting to flee the area before live rounds are fired.

The P.A. system rings out with instructions, "All inmates get on the ground. Shots will be fired."

The PA squawks again. In Spanish this time. It sounds like, "Questa say. Questa say, ma tusos!" At least that is what my brain registers as I throw myself to the ground.

Looking up from my prone position I see correctional officers, and other staff members, running toward the scuffle. More gunshots and the loud siren pierce the air like a broken record repeating the, "Get on the ground," instructions in both English and Spanish. Laying in the dirt I wish I had a battle helmet on. Adam interrupts my thoughts.

"Yo, Chad. Welcome to Vietnam my friend. Shit gets real around here. You have to get used to it, bro. It happens all the time around here, kid."

"This shit is crazy," I call back.

"Yeah, but it's always exciting, and it passes the time." He says.

If this is how they pass time around here, I think to myself, I am sure to see a lot of despair. I can only pray that I am not on the receiving end of "Passing Time."

After running into harm's way, the officers have quelled the assault. Creeper seems to be awake, but distraught. Blood flows from his face and his dirty, white t-shirt is adorned with red circles where his skin was punctured by the makeshift prison shanks. Those who committed the assault are handcuffed and escorted off the yard. Creeper is not cuffed, but he is led off the recreation yard by an officer who holds Creeper's hands behind his back.

My mind dances with thoughts while Adam talks to me. I hear him, but whatever he is saying does not register. My stomach seems to be twisting and turning like a whirlpool, as I realize that the thought of being shot did not deter these men from continuing their assault. The thought of being shot had no bearing on these deranged men.

I cry out silently to God for help. Where am I? Please, help me God!

Before long, a voice on the loudspeaker orders us to stand up, and to leave the yard when our housing unit is called. The recreation yard is officially closed for the evening; earlier than usual. No complaints from me.

As I make my way off the yard, I am sad. I think about how I would rather not smell fresh air, or have the wind beat against my back, or the rays of sun to beat on my face, if it comes at the expense of watching someone being stabbed and brutalized, while bullets whiz through the air.

On the way back to the housing unit, Adam tells me that he, "needs to talk to me some more in the morning." He also mentions that it is something important, and that he wants to introduce me to a guy named Dennis from Boston. We say our goodbyes with handshakes.

Paying heed to the wearing shoes to the shower instructions, I gather my hygiene products into a heap and beeline to the shower. I'm concentrating on Adams words, that he has to talk to me about "something important." What could be important? The word important sets my mind to juggling; worrying a little bit. Perhaps it is the extreme violence I witnessed that has me on edge.

Only time will tell...

CHAPTER

EIGHT

T HE MORNING COMES EARLY after a night of little rest. Different thoughts race through my mind like an out of control Amtrak train. That made sleep hard to come by. The assault on Creeper, and Adam's mention of having to talk to me about "something important" left me in a state of disarray. I wish that the Federal Bureau of Prisons would have me sent somewhere other than this magic mountain.

Kelly is the first person I see when I exit my cell. As has been the custom, we make our way to the mess hall together. Kelly tells me he is moving to another housing unit where some of his homeboys from his state are housed. The surprise, and disappointment, must be obvious on my face as it prompts Kelly to delve into one of his Prison 101 instructional talks.

We stop mid-stride. "Look here honkey," he says, with a serious face. "You got a forty piece. I ain't going to be here much longer anyway. You're gonna figure this shit out. You got no other choice Chad."

"I just wish you weren't moving though, for real." I say.

"You're cool. You been hanging out with Nick anyway. He's your homeboy. If you need me bro, I ain't that far from you. I'll see you on the yard everyday kid. You're supposed to meet Adam, and your homeboys today anyway, right?"

"Yeah, I think so," I respond.

"What the hell do you mean, you think so?" Kelly said

"Yeah, I'm meeting them today," I respond in a gloomy voice.

"Come on now Chad. Don't act like your fucking dog just died. Crackers crumble, honkeys rumble. You're a God damn honkey with forty years. That little kid, sad shit, ain't going to get it in here. It's man up time, my boy. So, what's up? You going to be alright right?"

"Man, I'm going to be alright," I say with false confidence in my voice.

Kelly reaches his hand out to shake mine and we continue to the mess hall. In a sense, Kelly was like a security blanket for me. Or a big brother in a place where very few people extend a hand to help with good intentions. Now after just a few days that blanket is being ripped from under me.

Eating breakfast is almost as difficult as sleeping was. We eat in silence while my nerves do somersaults. My stomach is uneasy. I shovel the food down tasting nothing. My focus is on Kelly moving, and me having to find my own way here at Big Sandy. Not knowing what the future has in store for me in this forsaken place rattles me. This is my journey—when I made a choice to sell drugs, I chose my path, and with it my destination. Whatever is going to happen here, I think to myself, is going to happen. Prison can be a frightful place. Adjusting takes time; eventually most people do. If you don't adjust, you perish.

My prison thoughts are halted when I see Adam in the distance coming through the kitchen doors. He's not alone. A small Irish kid, heavily tattooed with four leaf clovers, accompanies him as they approach me with Adam's outstretched hand.

"Chad, this is Dennis, the homeboy from Boston that I was telling you about." We shake hands as Dennis chimes in.

"We were waiting on you. Knew you was coming. What are you doing after breakfast?" His Boston accent is unmistakable.

"Nothing. Why what's up?"

"Come out to the yard so I can holler at you, bro," Dennis says with a smile.

"Alright," I answer, playing things cool. I take everything in little by little. My first impression of Dennis is that he is a tough, confident kind of kid about the same age as me.

Dennis tells me to wait until they get done eating and we will all shoot out to the yard together. "It's better to be together around here," he says with a sly smile.

Once Dennis and Adam finish eating, we walk to the yard. The fresh air seeps into my lungs. Birds chirp in the distance. The sun is warm. Peace blankets the yard. The battlefield from last night is no more, and I welcome the calmness. All three of us set out toward the track. Dennis initiates conversation.

As Adam looks on, Dennis tells me that in federal prison they have what the prisoners, and staff, call cars. A car is a group of men from a certain area. Dennis' car consists of White guys from the East Coast, mostly from Massachusetts and New York. He is adamant that the car is not a gang, but a group of men from the same area who have things in common, and who watch each other's backs. He goes on further: the White gang members at Big Sandy are oppressive and try to take advantage of White inmates who are on their own.

Taking advantage of White inmates who are on their own grabs my attention. Right now, I am on my own. Curiosity coupled with the fear of being taken advantage of prompts me to ask for details.

"What are the gang dudes doing?" I ask in my pretend nonchalant voice. In reality, I don't want anyone to know I am worried about being on my own and equally worried about these White gang members trying to turn me into a Big Sandy victim.

"All kinds of bullshit," Adam replies.

"The douche bags are cutting knives out of dudes beds," Dennis says. "Extorting good White dudes to feed their drug habits, stealing, and one dude was trying to rape a younger White dude. He ended up getting smashed the day you came in. We had a couple dudes punish him. He left on a stretcher."

I saw that guy leave on the stretcher, but I don't share that with

Dennis or Adam.

It's Adam's turn to speak. "We just came from Bloody Beaumont bro, down in Texas, and what we ain't going for are our people getting taken advantage of. We are putting our own thing together bro, and being you're from the Big Apple like me, this is your car—us—it's our car. This is your home. It's where you belong. You got a lot of time bro, and this is the wrong place to be alone." Adam says all this in a stern, almost urgent voice.

I am already convinced I know exactly what I am going to do even if I don't share it with either of them yet. Being alone, or on my own, behind these walls is not an option. If there is a sign-up sheet, I sure wish they would give it to me. The dotted line is surely calling my name. In my old life I was a tough guy, but this place is filled with a lot of guys tougher than me. In my heart I know I can hold my own one on one. Big Sandy is not a one on one type of place. The best choice for me is with my homeboys. At least that's what I think for the moment; for the here and now.

"These gang dudes are like vultures," Dennis adds.

"When we first got here, we almost went to war with the ABTs— the Aryan Brotherhood of Texas—but they didn't really want it," Adam says, excitement in his voice. "You see that dude over there? That's Dinky, their lame ass shot caller. He's a real dirt ball piece of White shit." I look off to my right in the direction Adam is pointing in. Standing there is a scraggly looking White prisoner. He is the same guy I met the day before who initially rubbed me wrong. "Dinky was scared to death. He knows we would have butchered him and his whole car. We had a hundred White dudes out here with vests on and bone crushers. It would have looked like the St. Valentine's Day Massacre, or the Attica Prison Riots out here. He wanted to politic it out. He wanted to talk things out," Dennis tells me.

I interrupt with what I can tell seems like a silly question to him.

"Listen man, I am new, so I don't know a lot. What the hell is a bone crusher and a vest?"

Dennis laughs. "Yeah Bro, you're green as fuck, and you got a lot to learn. A bone crusher crushes bones. You have to come to the unit later, and I'll show you what it is. We make vests out of the long sleeve shirts. We got guys that sew big pockets in them in the vital areas. Once the pockets are in, we put magazines and books in the pockets. If you get stabbed in that area, it protects your ass from dying in here."

"Damn man, this is a crazy place," is my response. My mind somersaults as each new piece of violence, or the potential for it, passes my ears.

My mind races as I realize more and more how serious USP Big Sandy really is. I try to play things off so both Adam and Dennis don't realize how nervous I really am about this place. For a moment, I am back in front of the mirror that morning I left Youngstown, Ohio. Once again, I am unsure if I am going to be okay.

I do not think there is much of a choice for me. It's either be in this car, or be here on my own, and being on my own does not seem feasible in this environment. The way Adam and Dennis laid things out reinforces my sudden desire to be a part of a car. It is clear to me that I am being recruited to be a part of this gang that these two guys have convinced themselves is not a gang. They simply switched the name from gang to car. Within days of being in prison, I am doing exactly what I had promised myself I would never do—join a gang. I reason within myself that I made that promise before I knew what prison was really like.

Both Mr. Young and Kelly warned me not to do this, but they must be wrong. *They have to be wrong,* I tell myself. If people who are on their own are being raped, having their stuff stolen, and having White, racist gang members cut knives out of their beds, why would I, or anyone, choose to be on their own in here?

"Chad, you're a homeboy no matter what. You're from New York. All we got in here is each other. You know we are going to have to check your paperwork to make sure you're a good dude. Once we check that you can get your driver's license. No offense to you it's just how it is," Adam says with a sly smile.

"Do you got your docket sheet, and sentencing transcript?" Dennis asks.

"I got that stuff in my property, and my PSR."

"You got your PSR in there?" Dennis asks surprised.

"Yeah, I got it." I said.

"They don't let us have them no more. Hopefully you got it hidden in there, and they give it to you bro." Dennis said.

"As soon as I get my property, I will make sure I get those papers to you," I say sternly. I feel myself getting a little more confident.

Adam interrupts my confidence, "Yah, once we check that out you get your license if everything checks out. And I got a knife for you." My newfound confidence disappears when he mentions the knife. I really don't want to be carrying a knife and, more than that, I don't want either Adam or Dennis to know. I keep this fact to myself. I can see I will need to keep many other things to myself.

"Tonight, after chow, you have to come to our unit. Come over to meet the homeys, check out the vests, and our arsenal." Dennis says this with bravado in his voice.

Looking for an excuse to not have to go to his unit, I ask, "How the hell am I going to get to your unit with the cop in there?"

"The cop doesn't care who comes into the unit, bro. He's doing his eight and going home," Dennis snickers.

"That bitch Adkins ain't working our unit tonight?" Adam asks.

"Nah bro. He's the two-day relief," Dennis says.

"Yah, you're good Chad. We'll see you after dinner bro," Adam says.

As I walk to my unit, I find myself shaking my head. I can't believe I made the irrational and irresponsible decisions that brought me to Big Sandy to meet Adam and Dennis. Tonight, dinner brings with it my introduction to vests, and sharpened metal for dessert.

NINE

DENNIS TAKES ME INTO HIS CELL. I feel a burst of adrenaline entering my veins ignited by the unknown. He opens his locker, then he removes a false shelf that reveals his small cache of prison weapons. Dennis first shows me a menacing piece of steel, about nine or ten inches long. I can see that the metal is from one of the beds, and I wonder if Dennis cut it from a bed belonging to one of the White guys who are on their own. Scanning his bunk, I can see no metal is missing from his bed. He hands me the shank. I inspect it. I am swollen with curiosity. Both sides are sharpened and meet at a threatening point that looks as if it can actually pierce a person's bones.

I can tell my fascination that something this dangerous can be fabricated in a prison cell shows on my face when Dennis says, "I told you bro, we got bone crushers in here."

I flip the make-shift weapon in my hand as I continue my examination. One end of this pointed dagger is wrapped in black electrical tape for better grip. There is a string tied in a small circle so it can be wrapped around the stabber's wrist. With the lanyard hooked around the combatant's wrist there is slim chance a prison warrior will lose this weapon during the fight.

Holding the shank in my hand, I cannot begin to fathom how it would feel to be on the receiving end of a stabbing by such a brutal weapon. There is no doubt that in the hands of a deranged prisoner this weapon could be used to send any one of the fifteen hundred prisoners at Big Sandy, including myself, to a tumbling, brutal death.

Dennis tells me he made this knife on his own. He took the guard off a pair of beard trimmers, and took a small nail clipper, and used them as saws. Armed with these tools he dug into the bed frame of another inmate's bed. After long hours of tedious sawing, he successfully separated a piece of metal from the bed frame. Once the metal was free, he spent hours sharpening the knife on a hard surface. Back and forth, over, and over, until he had the killing point he wanted.

I hand the knife back. Dennis smiles, showing me his stained teeth. "Shit ain't no joke is it bro?"

"Shit's real I see," is my response. Dennis continues, a mad concierge, proudly displaying the rest of the arsenal he told me about earlier. There are knives of all sizes coupled with grotesque metal bars. Some of the knives are made from Plexiglas stripped from fluorescent light fixtures in the cells, others were formed from melted plastic. Other bone crushers, smaller than the one I handled earlier were visible.

Figure 6 - More prison shanks.

Dennis picks up a piece of steel rebar pipe that's at least a foot long and heavy. He slaps it in his palm. Suddenly he takes a swing at the corner of his locker, startling me. Paint and small speckles of metal explode into the air on impact. My heart races and my adrenaline surges. The fight or flight instincts kick in. I wonder if I am safe.

The panic that has just set in is broken by Dennis' laugh. Dennis says, "This will break a mother fucker's head, bro. Put 'em out for the count."

Wanting to break my uncomfortableness, I reply, "Where did you get all this shit from man?"

"We got a dude in our car named Preston. He works in the kitchen, bro. Ripped like ten of them out of the ceiling."

I am surprised that a prisoner could simply rip ten bars of steel rebar out of a ceiling and somehow get them back to a housing unit. "You know if you hit someone in the head with one of them there is no question, you're going to kill him," I say.

Dennis takes me all the way back to fifth grade. "Duhhh. That's the point. Around here, we're playing for keeps. There are no tomorrows around here, bro. If one of these douche bags is stabbing you and you get a shot off to his dome with this, he won't be stabbing you no more would he, bro?"

"I guess not dude," I respond.

The captain was right when he told me to get a knife. Everyone in this place has one, or some sort of weapon. I debate whether I should have one, but debating does not make sense to me. It seems like decisions in here are made for me based on the circumstances that surround me.

"Yeah Chad, we never make bad decisions, and any mission we go on we always send three or four guys. We make sure we never lose, and I'm hoping you make the right decision here. Keeping it real, bro. In this place, your next move has to be your best move. There really is no room for mistakes. Me and you are about the same age, got the same time, so for real take my lead. All I am saying to you is to help you so you make it around here."

"Yeah, Dennis, I understand. I just got to get into the groove of things around here." I said.

"Come on bro, I am going to introduce you to the Big Homey, Stevie. He's from my neighborhood. Gots a life sentence, kid. For real. He has the keys to the car. We run a tight car in here. Stevie is at the top, and Adam is like the second in command."

Stevie looks to be in his mid-fifties. The man is completely bald—his body is decorated with all kinds of Celtic knot work representing his Irish heritage. He does not look like the stereotypical prison shot caller. He's not what I imagined. When Dennis was telling me about him, I had a much different image. I thought the guy would be a big, muscle-bound, Irish-looking guy. Stevie is small in stature, bald, no facial hair. He reminds me of Casper the Ghost.

Like many things in prison, looks can be deceiving. Mr. Young, my cellie, filled me in on some of Stevie's backstory prior to this meeting. His looks do not match his history. While he does not look dangerous, his résumé says he is. As it turns out Stevie is not serving one life sentence. Stevie is serving three life sentences. In the mid-'90s he and his counterparts were in the business of robbing armored cars. One of these robberies in the Boston area resulted in the death of a guard.

Mr. Young told me that it was also rumored that Stevie killed another inmate in a knife fight at United States Penitentiary Marion, Illinois. As a result of that killing, he was locked in a cage all by himself for five years. Being confined to a cell for five years all alone can only ignite one's hatred and anger. USP Marion was built in Illinois back in 1963. It was designed to replace the notorious Alcatraz prison, and was designed to house, "The Worst of the Worst," that the United States had. While Stevie was on that list, others much more dangerous roamed the confines of that prison. People like Thomas Silverstein, one of the leaders of the Aryan Brotherhood gang.

Silverstein is by far the most famous White prisoner the Federal Bureau of Prisons has ever held. In 1981, he was accused of killing another inmate by the name of Robert Chappelle. This was done by wrapping a wire around Chappelle's neck and strangling him through the cell bars while he lay sleeping. Less than a year later his murderous streak behind prison bars continued when he stabbed Raymond "Cadillac" Smith with a prison shank over sixty times, ending his life behind Marion's dark walls.

Cadillac had his own stature in federal prison. He was the shot caller for the D.C. Black gang. D.C. as in Washington, D.C. This is a group of prisoners who, to this day, are known for their unity as well as their penchant for trouble behind the razor wire.

Silverstein's thirst for violence in Marion did not end with the killing of two Black inmates. Just over a year after Cadillac's murder he struck again. This time the person in his sights was not a convict. This time he was a correctional officer. On a chilly October day in 1983, armed with his customary weapon of choice, Silverstein attacked Officer Merle Clutts. When the battle for life, or death, had ceased Clutts was on the losing end. He died in brutal fashion after being stabbed more than forty times.

Figure 7 - Corrections Officer Merle Clutts.

With three vicious murders under his belt at Marion, Silverstein's status as, "The Worst of the Worst," in the federal prison system shot to the top. Few federal inmates, if any, have surpassed his status to this day.

Clutts' murder would not be the only shocking thing that happened at Marion that October day. Eight hours after Silverstein struck, his good friend, and fellow prisoner, Clayton Fountain, was looking to make his own mark. Like Silverstein he armed himself with a sharpened death instrument.

This time correctional officer Robert L. Hoffman was on the receiving end of the beastly violence that plagued the Marion prison. Like Clutts, Hoffman met his maker on that dark October day.

Figure 8 - Corrections Officer Robert L. Hoffman.

Two guards had never been murdered on the same day in the same prison. As a result of the day's events, those in charge of the Federal Prison System made changes at Marion. The facility was turned into a lock down prison. All prisoners were to be locked in their cells twenty-three hours a day, seven days a week. Prisoners were permitted one hour a day, five days a week out of their cells for what, almost ironically, came to be known as "recreation."

This is where Stevie spent five years of his life. For many, this was part of his folklore; this seemed to bring many young White convicts into his fold. Regardless of his looks, I get the feeling that Stevie's disregard for the lives of others makes him dangerous. Being able to discern who is who behind these walls is a quality I am beginning to develop. Such a quality may turn out to serve me well in here.

Stevie tells me that both Adam and Dennis think I am a good guy, and that it would make him happy if I did the right thing by joining the car. I feel as if I am on the spot. I'm in a position where I have to make a decision and I'm not able to give it much thought. Stevie seems to have some magical, influential power, or spirit. He urges me to do what he calls the right thing. Within seconds an agreement to be a part of the car comes out of my mouth although my senses are tugging at me, an alarm within telling me to decline the offer at least for now. The word, "No," cannot be found. Stevie reaches out to shake my hand, pulling me into him with a hug, coupled with a pat on the back. I am now welcomed into this East Coast prison brotherhood with hugs from Adam and Dennis. They look at me with big smiles as if they just brought another soldier into their fold. They look at Stevie as if they are looking at him for the praise a small boy seeks from his father. In time I learn that all the guys in the car do whatever Stevie asks them to do. He has a leadership quality that most people long for, but never find.

After we leave the confines of Stevie's cell, Dennis explains that there is a probation period before I am fully accepted into the car. Guys that are new to the car are the ones that are called upon to "put in work," or to go on what are called "missions." When problems arise, probationers are the ones expected to wreak violence on any prisoners who transgress any of the prison rules set out in The Convict Code. This is the part where a person's loyalty to the car is tested. Some people will kill for their car. Whether it be out of fear, loyalty, or to enhance one's prison cred is a mystery to me, but at the end of the day this is the reality in a maximum-security prison.

Cars work in different ways behind these walls. Men within the cars are ordered to do things that will jeopardize them or place them in positions where they could end up with new charges. Sometimes it might be a simple assault. Other times they may be ordered to mule drugs on visits. Whatever the shot caller needs he asks for, and any objection is considered a disrespect to the car. The end result of any refusal is an assault on the objector. Saying no is a no-win situation.

If a shot caller likes a person, he might not call on that person to do his dirty work, but eventually everyone has to put in some work. Every car has expendables. These guys are referred to as missiles, or crash test dummies. Shot callers summon them to missions under the guise that they are putting in work for the good of the car. Victims of violence are usually people who are found out to be sex offenders, or those who snitched on someone at some point in their lives. Dennis explains all this to me, but assures me that because I am from New York, I am part of the upper echelon. This is when I learn there are others in the car who are not from the East Coast. Some are from the Midwest; some are from the South. These are our missiles. According to Dennis, "They're not really our home boys."

Tonight, the car is having a meeting. I am expected to be on the yard at six o'clock. The yard at night always leaves me with an unsettled stomach. For me, the yard is more of a gladiator pit than a place of recreation. I am not looking forward to this meeting but then again, who really is…

CHAPTER

TEN

Yeah, this album is dedicated
To all the teachers that told me I'd never amount to
nothin'
To all the people that lived above the buildings that I
was hustlin' in front of
Called the police on me when I was just tryin' to make
some money to feed my daughter (it's all good)
And all the niggas in the struggle
You know what I'm sayin'? It's all good
Baby Baby!
It was all a dream, I used to read Word Up Magazine.
Salt-n-Peppa and Heavy D up in the limousine
Hanging pictures on my wall
Every Saturday Rap Attack, Mr. Magic, Marley Marl
I let my tape rock 'til my tape popped...

MY ROAD TO BIG SANDY started in late 1994. Me and my friends would sit around a floor model television watching a fuzzy program called *The Juke Box*. We could call in and request songs that would be charged to one of my friend's grandmother's telephone account. We would order Biggie's "Juicy" back to back.

Like Biggie, it was all a dream. There were usually five of us watching Booper's Grandmother's floor model, while his mother was upstairs smoking cocaine base with Uncle Bobby. Booper's Uncle Bobby was a pimp and a drug addict who sold cocaine to support his own habit.

It wasn't long before me and Booper started putting together a plan—to get paid and "blow up" like the World Trade Center. We were fifteen but motivated by our circumstances. Poor White kids from the ghetto. We wanted more than we had. We stole empty cocaine bags out of Uncle Bobby's dresser and filled them with baking soda.

My career as a street hustler began when we passed off eleven bags of baking soda for cocaine to one of Bobby's customers. Before long, we were buying real cocaine in small quantities, and packaging it up in ten-dollar bags. We were becoming the guys we looked up to in our neighborhood—the hustlers, the cats standing on the corner, guns tucked in their waist, shooting dice, and selling cocaine all day. To us they were the villains, the heroes, the people we aspired to be. They had money, cars, nice clothes, women. We had nothing but beat up Starter jackets and ragged Bo Jackson series Nikes.

At fifteen, I wanted to be like the White kids from the suburbs. I wanted a car at sixteen. The difference between us and them—my single mother was just as broke as me. She was not buying me a car. I was determined to get my own.

Like Biggie, I was reaching for the stars. I cocked my Starter hat to the side and set out for the block with a pocket full of cocaine. Little did I know I was slowly walking my way from Rochester, New York to Inez, Kentucky.

ELEVEN

THE MEETING ON THE YARD is getting ready to begin. Different guys in the car greet each other with fist bumps and handshakes. Before long we all form a circle around Stevie. Stevie looks more and more like Casper the Ghost, especially under the lights as the night approaches. The meeting was supposed to be so all the guys can get acquainted with each other.

A quick head count tells me there are over seventy White guys in the car that I joined earlier. Like most things, the more one has, the stronger one is. In the prison context the more soldiers you have, the stronger your army. The stronger your army, the more influence you have.

As the men come together, Stevie calls for silence. Once he has the silence, he delves into a profanity laced tirade about how bad White gang members are. He tells us how they try to victimize "good White dudes" like all of us. Stevie tells us that if we did not have each other we would be victimized by these heathens who thrive on victimizing their own people while hiding under a phony cloak that they represent the White race and help Whites. I scan the men among me bobbing their heads in agreement to Stevie's every utterance. It looks like they are under a Jim Jones trance.

According to Stevie our car is the only car that has the men to stop the oppression because we have the numbers. He reminds me of Ronald Regan giving one of his great speeches before a crowd of onlookers. He knows how to engage his faithful minions, how to incite them with threats of fear from his opposition, and how to engage them to commit violence if the situation calls for it. It is easy to see that he has manipulated these men to believe that he is their king.

As the speech continues it becomes evident that this hatred is directed towards a guy from California named "Bam." Bam is the shot caller for the Aryan Brotherhood gang, which is by far the strongest White gang in the federal prison system.

The Aryan Brotherhood developed back in the 1970s as an organized predatory gang. The gang's main interest was protection, extortion, and narcotic sales in prison. This ruthless White gang also took on contract murders for other prison gangs, and individuals. The gang was merciless in the 1970s, with a reputation for being thirsty for blood. To this day they have a zero-tolerance policy for disrespect from others—staff and inmates alike. While they may not have the grip on the prison system they once had, they still have a mean reputation.

The Aryan Brotherhood lives by a Creed which says:

"An Aryan brother is without a care,
He walks where the weak and heartless won't dare
And if by chance he should stumble and lose control,
His brothers will be there to help reach his goal.
For a worthy brother no need is too great,
He did not but ask, fulfillments for his fate.
For an Aryan Brother death holds no fear,
Vengeance will be his, through his brothers still here.
For those Brotherhood means just what it implies,
A brother is a brother 'til that brother dies.
And if he is loyal and never loses faith,
In each brother's heart will always be a place.

So, a brother am I and always will be,
Even after my life is taken from me.
I'll lie down content, knowing I stood,
Head held high, walking proud in the Brotherhood."

This is a gang that was formulated on principles, a gang that had structure. Their penchant for violence only escalated their rise to notoriety. Serious members such as Tommy Silverstein would not hesitate to uphold their secret creed. Bam was cut from the same cloth as Silverstein. He held what Stevie aspired to possess: The Keys to the Yard.

Stevie wants to be the head honcho for all the Whites at Big Sandy. Bam is standing in his way. An obstacle to that ultimate goal. The agenda to take control is being pushed further every day.

Stevie begins to close. He tells us all, "Remember men, together we can conquer, but as individuals we will fail." This line must have been stolen from General Patton himself, or some other great military leader. He warns us that we are going to move on the White gang members soon. His speech has riled up the crowd. The convicts among me look thirsty for action with no regard for any consequences that might come from an attack on the gang members.

Before the meeting ends, Dennis grabs the floor. "You have two weeks to get your paperwork together," he tells all of us. "The car is having a paperwork party in the near future."

It is clear that in the event something goes wrong, the powers that be want to make sure that no snitches slipped into the car. Realistically though, with all the cameras in the prison worrying about someone telling on you in the event you kill another convict is a facade. The cameras are all that is needed.

Dennis continues. "You all need a knife. Everyone has to have at least one." For those who did not have a knife, he assured us that he had one for us once our paperwork checked out. All in all, Dennis is truly for the car. He believes in it, in the brotherhood. His aspirations are much like Stevie's. He wants to be the shot caller for the Boston car in prison. Prison is all he knows. Dennis walked in at the age of nineteen with a thirty-year sentence for robbing a hotel for less than $200, and a PlayStation.

Many of Dennis' hopes and dreams dissipated when the Judge handed down that thirty-year sentence, just like my own. He walked into prison a young man. His sad reality is that if he ever makes it out of prison alive, he will be leaving an old man with nothing in life. His story is the same as so many of ours—crushed dreams.

The faces of the men behind these walls tell the same story. There is not much to live for when your reality is coming to prison young and walking out old. Perhaps that is why the Aryan Brotherhood Creed says, "For an Aryan Brother death holds no fear." While the truth may not hit a prisoner right away, it happens eventually. When it does, it hits like a ton of bricks. Mine didn't happen when my Judge imposed my forty-year sentence. It was when I returned to my lonely cell that night that going to prison young and leaving old became my reality. In the back of my mind, I knew I had to do everything I could to change the trajectory of my destiny.

Prisoners deal with this pain, this despair, in different ways. Some opt for suicide, others numb the pain with drugs, some lash out with violence. Others just deal with it. Many in this position find something to hold onto. Dennis did that. He latched onto this make-believe car hoping he would be the shot caller someday. The car became his life. He was living for the car—nothing else.

The same could be said for Stevie. Life as he knew it was over with. Whatever prospect he once had of ever leaving prison a free man is gone, swept away like a rushing river with the denial of his last appeal. When he leaves prison, it will be in a body bag as a hearse delivers him to his final resting place. Stevie is the kind of man who has to control something. His mind would crumble otherwise. He had to formulate this car and elect himself the shot caller. To keep the car moving he has to create his own problems. This occupies his mind and keeps him from dwelling on his reality—the body bag and the hearse.

CHAPTER

TWELVE

"ONE OF THESE DAYS I'm going to tell you I told you so." Mr. Young turned to me while pouring a soda into a cup of ice.

"What do you mean by that?" I ask, with a little sarcasm in my voice. I roll my eyes slightly.

"Well, for starters, I see you out there with Adam, and them assholes. Mark my words, the last thing you need to do is, is get involved with them there degenerates."

"I just met those guys today."

"You must not remember when I pointed them guys out to you," he says. He continues without letting me answer him. "Don't get in that damn car if you ever want to make it off this mountain alive. If you don't listen to me, one of these days I am going to tell you I told you so."

My feelings tell me that Mr. Young is likely correct in his analysis, as well as his advice. A scolding from him is how my first night at Big Sandy started. Tonight is another night where his early to bed rule is out the window. It is clear that he despises Adam along with the rest of the car. He tells me that they all just came to Big Sandy from a prison in Texas, and that Stevie, Adam, and the rest of the crew think they are tough.

"If they think they are going to run this prison Chad, they are sadly mistaken."

"Why do you despise them so much?"

"Well, for starters they weren't here for a week before that Dennis and his buddy Ronnie beat up my old cell-mate."

"What did they do that for?" I ask with intent curiosity.

"For no God damn reason!" he says with anger in his voice. "He sat in a seat he has been sitting in inside the mess hall that they came here and claimed. They think they own those seats now. Them seats belong to Obama and Eric Holder, not the Boston, New York damn East Coast car or whoever they claim to be."

I smile pondering his statement about Eric Holder. Since he is the Attorney General, maybe he owns the seats after all. He is in charge of the Justice Department, and the federal prison system. If Mr. Young told the car that Eric Holder owned those seats, they would likely beat him up as well. More than half the guys in the car probably do not even know who Eric Holder is in the first place. But Mr. Young has no real power or say-so. They would kick his ass, old or not, if he expressed his opinion to anyone in the car.

"Let me tell you this young man, I have seen guys just like them a lot in this here prison. They don't last long. Those boys will be in more shit than Planters got peanuts."

This was the last thing I wanted to hear given my recent decision to join the car. I am deeply bothered by the fact that I pledged my allegiance to this car. With everything Mr. Young has told me, I cannot possibly tell him what I did. If I did, he would surely go off like a runaway train. Keeping this to myself seems like the better option.

I feel like a small child when the child knows he has done something wrong. Anxiety, confusion, and stupidity mix. As Mr. Young talks it feels like I am being scolded by my father and I'm trying to hide the shame of a bad choice. God only knows what I have gotten myself into. Jumping in headfirst was a mistake on my part, and deep inside I know it. As I drift off to sleep, I find myself anticipating my future here at

Big Sandy and wondering whether Mr. Young is going to tell me he told me so.

The morning arrives with the sun bouncing brightly off the window, illuminating the cell. Mr. Young rolls out of bed. I lay there silently making excuses to myself, contemplating the many bad decisions I've made over the course of my young life. Joining this car triggered regrets. Feeling sorry for myself will accomplish nothing. I shake the thoughts from my conscious mind and slide out of bed to begin my day.

At breakfast I find myself with my newly acquainted car members. Reality sets in quickly. Most of these men are living in a fantasy land. It is apparent we are all caught in some phony prison movie where the script is already written. I ponder that thought. There is a fake bravado of being a tough guy. Many men pretend to be something they are not. It becomes obvious that many prisoners are faking it to make it. Behind these walls hardened men seem to create their own problems, to make trouble with other prisoners over things that would be trivial in society.

It seems absurd that a person would want to create a hostile environment for themselves, an environment riddled with violence, but that is what happens on this side of the razor wire. There are men here who are truly barbaric, hateful, and cold-hearted but many of the guys are simply pretending. In order to survive you have to play the prison game the way it exists. A game in which the rules change daily. Joining the car was the first move in the prison game for me. When Dennis was recruiting me, he told me my next move had to be my best move. Because I was a younger White guy from New York, there really was no choice. Had I refused the offer they would have sent missiles to attack me. This is something I would later learn. There is no choice with the East Coast car. You're either in, or you're out of here. The only way you leave is as a victim of violence.

In Convict Code this is called, "beating someone off the yard." Once a group of prisoners assault a prisoner, that prisoner is no longer safe in population. The Bureau of Prisons will then transfer that prisoner to another prison to start anew.

At breakfast, I meet a guy named Ace. He is the shot caller for the Ohio, White Independent car. Ace and his comrades have an alliance with our car. Like Stevie, he has a hatred for White gang members. Arrogance rolls off him as he tells me his story. For Ace, his future holds nothing but this crazy world. He was in his twenties when he was sentenced to over two hundred years for robbing banks. His future holds nothing but anguish and despair. You can almost see it in his eyes when he speaks. For him, the free world was like the Titanic—sunk on that cold night. Like Stevie he latches onto the car. It's all he has left. Having the keys to the Ohio car is his safe haven. That safe haven does not last long for Ace at Big Sandy.

Months later, members of his own car find him to have committed one of the ultimate prison sins. Some time ago, Ace was put in the Special Housing Unit (SHU pronounced "shoe") for assaulting another prisoner. While in the SHU, he accepted a Black prisoner from Ohio as his cell mate. Once Ace served his time in the SHU he was returned to General Population. A plot has been put into place to beat him off the yard.

The yard seems still. Most people know what is going to happen, or at least they thought they knew. Two young White convicts from Ohio are stalking Ace. A tall, White kid named Slim, the other a stocky blonde with tattoos on his face. Ace has his back to the two villains and is engaged in a heated verbal dispute with another Ohio prisoner. Slim sneaks up behind him and swings for the fences. Slim's first punch crunches with the impact, landing to the side of Ace's face. Tattoo Face begins to swing wild, glancing blows as Ace ducks, dodges, and pulls a prison shank from his waist.

Tattoo Face sees the knife, and bolts from the scene leaving Slim to his demise. Ace is stabbing Slim. The two bodies lock up, and fall to the ground. Slim is on the bottom, his hands flailing as Ace mounts him. The sirens blare out. The loudspeaker instructs everyone to get on the ground. A warning shot reverberates off the concrete walls as Ace slashes downward with his sharpened bone crusher. Another warning shot does not deter the onslaught of violence. Slim fights for his life.

The correctional officer in the gun tower sets his sights at center mass. Once his target is set, he pulls the trigger sending the bullet from an AR-15 assault rifle into Ace's body. Immediate impact. Ace topples over the lanyard holding his shank in place. Slim scrambles to his feet sucking in air. He darts from the area where he almost lost his life. Confusion engulfs the yard as panic sets in among both staff and convicts.

Seeing Ace shot radiates the reality that losing your life is a real possibility. It is not going to always be warning shots. Staff members are coming from everywhere. Medical personnel with red medical bags rush to Ace and roll him over onto his back. One nurse seems to be brushing dirt off what looks like his intestines seeped out of the gaping hole in his stomach. Ace is staring into the sky as if he sees Satan's Angels coming to take him to purgatory. The nurse is pushing his intestines back into his body. It is too late for Ace; his blood will forever be left on the razor wire here at Big Sandy. Another inmate met his maker on the prison yard.

Violence has claimed Ace's life. His car, the car that he held onto so dearly was his demise in the end. His two hundred year sentence began, and ended, behind these gloomy concrete walls. Ace is loaded on a stretcher. The wind dances through the razor wire.

Nineteen percent of all male inmates in U.S. prisons say they have been physically assaulted by another inmate. Big Sandy is known for housing some high-profile inmates. The prison houses a significant portion of the people convicted of crimes in the Washington, D.C. area. The National Capital Revitalization and Self-government Improvement Act of 1997 gave the Federal Bureau of Prisons custody of sentenced D.C. felons. About thirty-three percent of the inmates here at Big Sandy have been convicted of D.C. crimes. The D.C. car is the biggest car at the prison. When a car has numbers, they wield the power on this side of the razor wire. While many men are here pretending, some have learned to become violent. Others are simply brutal.

October and November seem to be the months when Satan hovers over the prison. In October 2006, thirty-three-year-old Terrell Johnson, serving a sentence for armed bank robbery, stabbed fellow prisoner, Calvin Speight, in the neck with a bone crusher. Speight, like Ace, met his maker in Inez, Kentucky. Two years later, Johnson pleaded guilty to a charge of second-degree murder and was sentenced to a further twenty-six years in prison. Fourteen years less than my forty-year term for a non-violent drug crime. When I hear Johnson's sentence come across my radio I simply shake my head.

Less than a month after Speight's murder, Shamoni Peterson met his end after a brutal beating by Darryl Milburne, and Dwaune Gravely. Milburne, Gravely, and Darone Crawford were all living in a SHU cell designed for two. On November 12, 2006, a corrections officer asked if they would accept a fourth cell mate. That fourth man was Shamoni Peterson.

Gravely, a senior member of The Bloods, and Milburne, decided to accept Peterson as a cell mate, but for only one reason—they wanted blood. Gravely believed Peterson had snitched on The Bloods and snitching comes with severe consequences. Soon after Peterson entered the cell, Milburne put a t-shirt over his mouth and suffocated him while Gravely beat him. Peterson was found dead the next morning. The trio kept the dead body in the cell with them all night while they plotted how to explain his death.

Violence is expected here, by both staff and inmates. On November 4, 2007, extreme violence erupted again when Eric Eymard repeatedly stabbed his cellmate in the neck with a prison made knife. After the assault, Eymard told staff that he had intended to kill his cellmate. His cellmate required surgery and hospitalization. Eymard's streak of violence did not end with the stabbing of his cellmate. That was just the beginning. While he was being prepared for transportation to a Federal Court to answer for the stabbing, he stabbed two correctional officers with a sharp weapon he fashioned from plexiglass.

Prisoner Steven Michael Reid, angry at his unit manager, decided to throw scalding hot water in his face. The unit manager ran out of the unit with first and second degree burns to his face, neck, and chest. Reid's transgressions came with an additional twenty-year sentence from a Federal Judge in Kentucky.

October 21, 2008, another federal prisoner from the New York area stabbed a prison guard over ten times in the head, back, and arm with a prison made weapon.

In November 2008, Big Sandy prisoner Aaron Pike was stabbed by White gang members over thirty times. Pike was stabbed in the face, hands, and back. When the carnage had come to an end, both hands were broken, both lungs were punctured, and Pike was Mercy Flighted, fighting for his life. Miraculously, doctors were able to save him.

Death is a constant at Big Sandy. 2009 was rung in with the murder of Vincent Earl Smith, Jr., a D.C. prisoner. John Travis Millner, who had been recently transferred to Big Sandy from USP Lee in Virginia for stabbing another prisoner, decided to stab his cell mate with a prison-made icepick before strangling Smith, Jr., to death.

Millner was at Big Sandy serving a life sentence for killing sixty-eight-year-old Church Trustee, Walter Coates, in a random shooting. Seeking the death penalty for prison killings is a rarity, but in 2013 the Justice Department was weighing whether to seek his execution.

J.M. Stepp's *Eden* was being transformed into *Humanity's Hell*, day after day, year after year. The violence, the death, the fear, will never end until Big Sandy ceases to exist. With each assault, every murder, I know my life is on the line. I stare at the sun sparkling off the razor wire wondering if my blood too will be left here. Only time will tell.

CHAPTER

THIRTEEN

Smokin' weed in Bambú, sippin' on Private Stock
Way back, when I had the red and black lumberjack
With the hat to match
Remember Rappin' Duke? Duh-ha, duh-ha
You never thought that hip-hop would take it this far
Now I'm in the limelight 'cause I rhyme tight
Time to get paid, blow up like the World Trade
Born sinner, the opposite of a winner
Remember when I used to eat sardines for dinner
Peace to Ron G, Brucie B, Kid Capri
Funkmaster Flex, Lovebug Starski
I'm blowin' up like you thought I would
Call the crib, same number, same hood, it's all good
And if you don't know, now you know, nigga
You know very well
Who you are...

"**Y**OUR FATHER'S A VICIOUS CRACKHEAD," Booper ragged as we sat at his grandmother's table bagging up the first ounce of cocaine we ever bought. "Juicy," was playing on the floor model.

"Fuck you. Your mother's a crackhead too," I replied. We both laugh in our ignorance.

My heart flutters from the nervousness and excitement that comes with bagging up cocaine. I sit at the front of the table so I can see the front door in case someone tries to come in and take our hard-earned product. Within days, we went from a fake product to a real ounce of cocaine. Half for Booper, half for me. Two glass plates sat in front of us. We took razor blades to the shiny rocks.

As I chopped the rocks into smaller dosages, I thought about all the money I wanted to make, the new Starter jacket I would buy, and the matching pair of brand-new Bo Jacksons. Money would help me escape my loneliness. It would help me buy the happiness I desired. The possibility that I could lose my life over ten-dollar bags of cocaine was never even considered. Losing my drugs was impossible. I was starting my rise to the top. In my stupidity, I never even thought that prison was possible. I was too smart to get caught, or so I thought.

Once our product was packaged, we headed out to a corner where there was a house that people were selling their own drugs from. Me and Booper had been out there stealing their customers for days. When one of the addicts would pull up, we would call to them before they went to the door. Most of them would come to us but some of the loyalists went to the door.

It was not long before one of the loyalists told the guy on the other side of the door what we were doing. That's when Coolie came out of the door with a pistol in his hand.

"You bitch ass mother fuckers stealing my customers?" he yelled as he fired a shot in the air.

We ran through the snow, hopping fences, racing back to the safe confines of Booper's grandmother's house, and the floor model. Sitting in front of the floor model we contemplated our next move. I knew I wanted that Starter jacket and new Nikes but now the plans had to change. If we were to continue in this business I knew we both needed a gun.

"We need pistols Booper. That's what we need—two burners man."

"Yah, we ain't letting his bitch-ass run us off. Those are our customers now," Booper replied.

The street hustling life was taking off. Full throttle. For the mean time we were going to sell cocaine to Booper's uncles' customers.

Don't let 'em hold you down
Reach for the stars
You had a goal
But not that many
'Cause you the only one....

I fell asleep on Booper's couch smiling, dreaming about reaching the stars like Biggie said.

CHAPTER

FOURTEEN

THE MORNING IS NEW with the sun shining bright. I tuck my commissary items away and put my radio in my pocket. I contemplate going outside. Perhaps I should stay inside. Part of me wants to stay inside to keep watch over my locker, the other part of me wants to go to the yard to taste the fresh air. Fresh air is a small thing to most, but I look forward to it. The stale air contaminated with cigarette smoke, and the dirty smell of sweat pushes me towards the hallway. I convince myself that my commissary will still be in my locker when I return, but I really have no idea if it will be. I am unsure if people are stealing here.

Outside, I have to pass through a metal detector. The detector is not plugged in. The correctional officer assigned to man the machine and ensure no inmates take bone crushers, or steel, to the yard is oblivious to the fact that there is no power. He's more concerned with a conversation he is engaged in with a petite nurse. The conversation might be his way of avoiding a confrontation with any convicts transporting weapons to the yard. One man after another passes through the detector without a single beep. How many men have weapons on them is anyone's guess.

The handball court seems to be calling me. When I was younger, I spent some of my summers playing the game on the back wall of my middle school. Two Mexican guys I came on the bus with are playing one on one. Both are Sureños, or South Siders as they are sometimes called. They are soldiers for the Mexican Mafia. Both the Sureños and the Mexican Mafia are highly respected by the staff and convicts alike. They are known behind these walls as well as outside of them as being a serious gang that has no qualms about using serious violence to meet whatever objectives their gang has.

The Mexican Mafia was first formed in the 1950s with a group of thirteen Mexican inmates at a prison in California. Those thirteen men banded together to protect one another from other prisoners at the facility. In an attempt to squash the newly formed gang, prison authorities began sending the original members to other prisons. Rather than squashing the gang, what authorities did allowed the founders of the gang to recruit new members at other prisons, strengthening the gang. Once members were released from prison the gang flourished in the free world, gaining even more strength and a stronger reputation.

All Sureños aspire to become Mexican Mafia members someday, so they can get a black hand tattooed on their chest with an M in the middle. Such a tattoo is a badge of honor, and with it comes power, and prestige, in the criminal world.

When it comes to Mexican gangs, the Mexican Mafia is at the top of the food chain. A 1992 movie titled *American Me* focused on the formation of the Mexican Mafia or the "Le Eme" as it's also known. Another movie *Blood in Blood Out* was loosely based on the gang architects, one of whom was "Peg Leg Morgan," a White man who adopted the Mexican way of life.

Not happy about the organization being put on display, the Mexican Mafia had two of the consultants on the *American Me* movie killed. Charles "Charlie Brown" Marquez and Ana Lizarraga were both shot to death. No one is off limits when the gang feels disrespected. No one.

Sad Boy, and Droopy invite me to play. Had I been Black they would have never made the invite. The Sureños have a strict code in here. They stay away from doing business, or associating, with Blacks as much as they can. Almost everyone in prison has a name other than their real name. Sad Boy does not look sad, yet this is what people call him. Droopy on the other hand, has a droopy kind of look. There are many characters in here. From Half Dead to Droopy, people from all over the country now confined in this desolate place.

Playing handball takes me out of prison. It is another activity in here that puts me in a pleasant place from my past. For the moment, I am on the back wall of my middle school with two friends. Droopy becomes Freddy, Sad Boy is Andy. I trick myself. When I do this, I am able to leave prison. Leaving takes away the pain of my reality. Today is not today, at least not right now.

Adam is standing off to the side of the court. I hadn't noticed him until now. When the ball goes out of play, he tells me he needs to talk to me after the game. For some reason him wanting to talk to me angers me. Maybe it's because talking to him pulls me from middle school back into prison. After the game I shake hands with the Sureños, thank them for inviting me to play, and walk toward Adam.

Adam extends his hand to shake mine. "What's up Chad?"

"Nothing much, what's up with you?"

"Ahh man, just out here strolling. Noticed you playing handball with the Mexicans. It's alright bro to play handball with the Mexicans, but you should try to find some White dudes to play with. Some guys in the car." He says this looking into the distance behind his sunglasses.

"I'm am not really on that racist shit," I respond.

"Nah man. Me either bro. It's just a better policy. Sometimes sports can get heated, competitive at times, and can lead to problems. One problem with another race could cause us all problems."

I nod in agreement but my anger builds.

He continues, "I ain't trying to do your time bro. Just trying to help you. Just a better policy to do things with your own. You're new to prison Chad, and there are a lot of things you're going to learn. Most of them you won't like, but some of these policies might save your life. Those Mexicans would kill you without a second thought, trust me."

To a certain extent, Adam might be right, but being from New York, I had friends that were Black, White, and Hispanic. New York is filled with people of different cultures, races, and languages. My best friend, and co-defendant, was of mixed race—Mexican and Irish. Now my way of thinking has to change. Prison, or Big Sandy, is a brand-new beast. One I am unfamiliar with.

"This prison shit is crazy." I say.

"I don't make the prison rules, or politics. I just follow them Chad. It's better for all of us that way."

"It's all good," I agree.

Adam and I shake hands parting ways. Once back at the Country Cottage, as I have been referring to my cell given all of Mr. Young's knick-knacks that adorn our housing area, I open my locker. My commissary items are still there. Mr. Young's angry look prompts me to initiate a conversation.

"What's up Mr. Young?" I ask.

"You just ain't going to listen are you boy?" he snarks. "I seen you out there with them guys again."

"What guys?"

"Oh, don't play stupid with me, young man."

"What the hell do you mean?" I ask.

"You was out there hanging out with that long hair fella. What the hell's his name… Adam, yah and he ain't nothing but trouble."

"I was playing handball and he wanted to talk to me," I try to explain but it's useless.

"I'm going to tell you I told ya so when something bad happens with you. And if you're in the hole, and I don't get to see ya, you just remember what Ol' Man Mr. Young told ya."

There is an overwhelming feeling that floods my inner self, telling me that the old man is probably going to be correct with his advice.

Mr. Young's scolding makes me feel like a kid. He has been here a lot longer than me, and I am sure he knows more than me. Mr. Young is wise in both years, and prison experience.

Feeling like I still have to explain myself, I respond, "Mr. Young, I am just trying to be cool with everyone. I ain't trying to offend no one."

"Well, for your sake, hopefully you won't be cooling off in the morgue with a toe tag on for messing with those scum bags," he says, raising his voice a little.

"Hopefully not."

"Yah. What would your mother say if she got that phone call?" he asks.

"Look you're an old man, and I'm not going to argue with you or talk about this bullshit."

"Think about your mamma, before you make a bad choice," he hollers out to me as I walk out of the cell. I don't know if I am mad at Mr. Young, or at myself, for making foolish decisions. The toe tag comment, coupled with the phone call to my mother statement, have my insides in an uproar. Standing against the wall I pretend to watch television while I envision a morgue. There I am. I'm looking at myself on a cold slab of stainless steel with a toe tag, and stab wounds. My mother crying with a phone to her ear.

The thought of dying in this place is real. My mother getting the call hurts me more than the dying part. If it were not for my mother, maybe the dying part might be better than serving a forty-year sentence.

Avoiding Mr. Young for the rest of the day is easy, but I cannot escape being locked in the cell at night with him. Once the doors lock, he begins...

"Chad, I don't mean to be hard on ya, and this is prison, I ain't supposed to be in no one's business, but you being young and new to prison, I am trying to help you."

"Nah, I understand." There is no reason for me to argue with Mr. Young, or to make excuses. I know he is right about everything he told me.

"I am telling you this prison is not like any other prison you ever seen Chad."

As I lay in my bed listening to Mr. Young, I find it hard to believe that my life has been reduced to living in a locked concrete bunker with another man three times my age, and a toilet, wondering if my mother might get that call.

CHAPTER

FIFTEEN

L IVING THE STREET LIFE comes with consequences. For me, those consequences came with a severe sentence, and my placement in a prison where my life could be taken at any moment. Feeling the need to be alone with my thoughts, I opt for the yard this morning. Mornings are the one time where there is peace here at Big Sandy, as most of the convicts are required to be at their jobs. Being new, no job assignment has been made for me, and with a forty-year prison term, a job is the last thing I want. Guys in here work eight-hour days, five days a week for about twenty-dollars a month, on average. For some convicts, jobs pass the day. I would rather pass my day playing handball or walking the track.

My hope is that today will be better than yesterday. Some of my uneasy tension has become a bit suppressed with the realization that this is my life. Every morsel of Big Sandy is a part of my life now. From the violence to the razor wire, it is all part of me. I earned it according to my sentencing judge. Forty years in Big Sandy was sufficient for my non-violent drug conviction. Some days I feel like I don't give a fuck about anything. It is usually the days when I replay my sentencing day. The day when my mother disappeared and left me wondering if I would ever see her again. Reality is, I have to be here. Making the best of it is the only option.

There are more people on the yard today than usual. My peaceful walk alone with my thoughts fade quickly as I easily recognize that there is tension on the yard. The tension is so thick you can cut through it with a knife. Already my prison instincts are coming to fruition. One of the most important tools I have learned within the first few days of being here is that I must be observant. Being able to recognize everything going on around me is one key to surviving in this hell hole.

Scanning the yard like a hawk soaring over an open field looking for prey I notice Mexican prisoners forming small groups around the yard. This world I now live in is a dog-eat-dog world, filled with lions, and hyenas, with very few zebras. Deep discussions are being had between the shot caller for the Sureños and some of his soldiers. My secret hope is that whatever problem is afoot has nothing to do with Whites, and Mexicans. There are about twenty White convicts on the yard, including me, compared to at least seventy-five Mexicans. We would get slaughtered. Thinking back to what Adam told me about the Sureños, I know every one of them is likely armed with a shank. This thought convinces me that as much as I might not want a knife, it may very well be time to get one and keep it on me at all times. Being here in Big Sandy I know now that I would rather get caught with it than not with it.

As the thought filters through my subconscious, I find out the problem with the Sureños has nothing to do with the Whites when a large, Mexican soldier grabs one of his comrades from behind in a choke hold. The victim is another Sureño, named Nokie, who also lives in the same unit I am housed in.

More Sureños circle Nokie. They deliver punches to his head, face, and body. Before long, he is rendered unconscious. The large Mexican lets Nokie's limp body fall aimlessly to the ground. Other people join the fray dishing out powerful kicks to Nokie's head, and body. One of the kicks wakes Nokie from his comatose state. Using the nearby fence, his fingers lock onto the shiny metal fence as he pulls his body up.

Finding his feet, he stumbles on a large push broom. Fighting for his life, he begins to swing the broom like Barry Bonds on steroids chasing the home run record.

"Come on puto," Nokie screams like a wild animal, as the warm blood runs down his face.

One of the soldiers rushes in, swinging wildly. Nokie's swing connects perfectly with the side of the combatant's head. Watching the first guy fall sends Nokie into a raging fury. He backs up to the fence yelling profanities in Spanish. His swinging intensifies in barbaric nature. Four men rush him at the same time. The broom connects with the side of one of the attackers. This slows Nokie down. The others pounce on him like mountain lions on a fawn.

The alarm finally goes off ordering everyone to the ground. Most of the prisoners comply, but not the combatants. Once again, Nokie is on the ground. The broom is now being used on him. Both Spanish and English are blaring out of the speaker ordering all the prisoners to the ground when the first gunshot rings out warning the soldiers that live rounds will be coming if the brutal assault does not cease.

BANG, BANG. I feel an explosion.

Officers circle the Sureños. Small black balls sail through the air hitting everyone in the vicinity. One man screams. I look up, shielding my eyes. I think he is shot, but no. Concussion grenades are being deployed to break up the melee. Another one explodes and I cover my head with my arms. Warning shots ring out again from the guard towers. Officers enter the gladiator pit, tackling the men to the ground with no remorse. I envision some old clips of the 1970s Pittsburgh Steelers defense. One man is picked up and body slammed. Another grenade comes flying down from the guard tower. It explodes in the air sending little black balls everywhere. They are ricocheting off the ground, off the handball walls, flying everywhere with no intended target. Whoever gets hit, gets hit. The balls do not discriminate.

The guard towers stand over thirty feet high. Sharpshooters are stationed in each of the seven towers. I cover my head with my arms.

I'm face down on the ground. My only hope is that I am not hit by a live round if those start flying. With staff in the area, I'm probably safe, though. Usually when correctional officers are in the area, the cops in the gun towers refrain from letting real bullets fly. I am thankful that staff has arrived, and that with their arrival my chances of being accidentally shot have diminished.

Had staff not arrived when they did there is no doubt in my mind that someone would have been shot. These combatants had an order from the shot caller to complete a mission—assaulting Nokie until he died, or until the cops arrived to stop them. The attackers had no intention of stopping. Even the gunshots did not deter them. The threat of possible death meant nothing. In the real world, the thought of getting shot, or killed, would be a deterrent. In here, the real world has long been forgotten by these men. When you are in a place like this with a sentence of forever, death becomes a welcoming thought. Once everything is lost there is nothing left to live for. There is no fear of death.

A man with a life sentence has been through so many ups and downs on that long criminal justice rollercoaster that no emotions remain. With sentences ranging from thirty years to life, there is nothing left that can be done to hurt the man who has been stripped of life, liberty, and the pursuit of happiness. That man sees death the same way a Muslim martyr does. The hope is that there will be something better on the other side of the rainbow because this side has nothing but suffering, pain, and loneliness.

Fuck rainbows, I don't like them no more.

Many people like me are serving draconian sentences for non-violent drug offenses. What is mindboggling to me is that while these forty-year sentences for non-violent drug crimes are being handed out, the average sentence in federal court for murder is twenty-two years. Had I killed someone, I would likely have been sentenced to eighteen less years.

The federal criminal justice system no longer has a parole system. When that door slams behind every prisoner with a crucial sentence, there are only two ways out of here, winning relief in court, or a body bag. Sadly, most people will leave here in a body bag. With my sentence, if I behave, I will get about five years off my term. Instead of getting out at sixty-four years old, I can get out at fifty-nine years old. That truth disturbs me.

With no incentive to do the right thing, many of the men around me become vultures, living a barbaric life, riddled with anger, and violence on an astronomical level. Behaving yourself in prison is almost impossible because other prisoners' actions dictate your reactions. Those reactions might require a person to stab the other person. Sometimes those reactions don't leave a person any choice. The prison machine is designed in such a way that it applies oppression. It's designed so the prisoner never wins. It's designed so the prisoner always loses.

Like with Nokie. He was fighting for his life. Had he simply not fought back he would certainly have died. Once he fought back, he earned a write up for fighting. There is no such thing as self-defense in prison. Once a prisoner starts swinging, he loses twenty-seven good conduct days, on average. When Nokie gets back from the hospital he will be taken in front of a disciplinary hearing officer. That's his reward for fighting for his life. He will now have to spend twenty-seven more days in prison where any one of those days could be his last. His gang will no longer want him after the brawl. Nokie is a marked man. A man marked by one of the most vicious prison gangs in the system, the Sureños.

Nokie's provocation was a common one. He owed the Crips for heroin. Owing money to the Blacks is not allowed by the Big Homey—the man who calls the shots for the gang. Nokie has two yard violations. He was dealing with the Blacks, and he couldn't pay his debt. In order to avoid a physical conflict with the Crips, the beating was on full public display. "Hands laid, debt paid," is a common theme in here. The debt was paid with Nokie's blood, kind of like Christ paying the debt of sin on the cross. In Big Sandy, the sinners keep sinning.

Nokie, like many before him, and many who will come after him, allowed his heroin addiction to get out of control. His tab kept riding higher with his need to get high. Knowing he could not pay never dissuaded him. The thought of getting hurt or killed did not override his hunger to let the fish swim through his veins.

The heroin told him, "Follow me, everything is alright." Kind of like that Uncle Kracker song, "Follow Me."

When the Crips had enough of the false promises of payment being made, they went to Nokie's shot caller. They knew that the only payment they would see would be blood, and they likely enjoyed that prospect. When assaults like the one on Nokie happen, it is akin to the spectators at the old Roman Gladiator pits cheering for the victim to be finished. Most of the men here enjoy seeing a good, violent scuffle, although they secretly pray they are never on the receiving end.

Had the Crips taken it upon themselves to assault Nokie, the whole yard would have erupted like a festering volcano. It would have created a full-fledged war between the Hispanics and the Blacks. Such a war would have reached every other maximum-security prison in the federal system that houses Sureños and Crips.

The easiest way to settle the dispute was to punish Nokie by vicious means. His death, or his transfer to another facility after his physical discipline evened the score. Dealing with the Blacks, owing a debt to them ensured he was ostracized from his gang. For the rest of his time in prison he is a marked man.

Another unwritten rule in here is that you never stop beating, or stabbing, another prisoner until either staff intervenes, or you kill the person. This is how every car, group, or gang operates.

One thing that I am intrigued by is why Nokie's gang brothers allowed him to get so far in debt, knowing the end result was going to be an attack like this. My guess is the people who knew were getting high with him. The others had no money to pay for the heroin, but Nokie had both the balls to deal with the Blacks, and enough swagger to convince the Crips that he had money—at least initially. The cycle of prison life is vicious like a pack of hungry wolves in Yellowstone National Park searching for vulnerable prey.

Two hours of laying on the hard-concrete causes pain to creep into the muscles of my legs. Some of the men are laying on their backs enjoying the warm summer sun. Others are talking amongst themselves. I too have changed my position to ease my discomfort. On my back now, I stare into the deep blue sky, tricking myself into believing that I can see Jesus Christ's face in the clouds. For a second, I whisper a plea for freedom to Him. I blink my eyes a few times, and He's still there in the clouds. It's almost as if He is smirking at my request. I snicker at the absurdity of it, that I think I see Him. Or maybe my snicker is because of the absurdity of Him granting me freedom from here. Hell, He could have intervened a long time ago, and put it in one of the juror's hearts to vote to acquit me. He could have put it in all their hearts. Instead, He decided to send me to Big Sandy with a forty-year sentence so He could sit in the clouds laughing at me.

Whether He is really there in the clouds or not, I throw a middle finger to the laughing cloud. "Fuck you," I mouth silently. "This ain't funny."

Before I can say anything more, officers are ushering us up to our feet. Brushing the dirt off the front of my pants, I scan the yard. The other men are grateful that they can finally stretch their legs out. As we head back to the housing units, I look back one last time before I walk through the doorway. He is there. In the clouds again laughing at me.

CHAPTER

SIXTEEN

"COME ON CHAD, I need your help with something," my neighbor Red says.

"What do you need my help with?" I ask

"Just come on, I'll show you."

I walk into Red's cell. It's extremely hot. Wires are dangling off the wall, there is a mop bucket on the floor with a plastic bag inside it, another mop bucket has a bag filled with homemade wine. Red has had this concoction brewing for three or four days. Everyone has a hustle. Red is turning wine into moonshine. This is how he pays for his heroin addiction.

Red is from North Carolina. A few years back he was sentenced to twenty-one years in federal prison for being a convicted felon in possession of a hunting rifle. He is a kid of many talents. Not only does he make moonshine, or White Lightning as it is called here, he also runs a makeshift tattoo parlor from his cell, a Walkman repair shop, and a greeting card factory. Every penny he earns goes into his veins.

Red wants me to help him distill his wine, a job I really don't want to be involved in. Things don't look safe in his cell.

"Look I am going to wrap these wires here to the wires in the light socket," he tells me. "If the electricity hits me, you got to grab me. Hit me. Just get me off the wires."

The look on my face does something to him because he starts to laugh hysterically at me. For some reason I do the same. "Fuck no, I ain't doing that." I say in disbelief, incredulous that he would ask me to do such a thing.

"Ahh man, you're one of these uppity honkeys from New York, think you can't make your own whiskey."

"Nah, I just ain't messing with no electric, and if your ass gets electrocuted, they ain't blaming me for killing your ass," I reply.

"So, you're going to let me get electrocuted bro?" Red asks, as he begins twisting the wires together with no regard to my objections. He starts laughing again. "If you ain't finna get me off this electric, and I die, I get an early release," he continues.

"Come on Red, I ain't with this shit man," I say making my way toward the door. Red starts shaking. I feel instant panic well up inside me. I want to dart for the door. I am halted by another of Red's hysterical laughs.

"I'm just fucking with ya man, I do this shit all the time."

"Man, you should not be playing like that Red."

"Don't trip it's all good. Just wanted to see if you were willing to try and save my life. I see you're not." He says with a giggle.

"Come on, I ain't messing with no electric kid."

"I can see that. With friends like you who needs enemies." We both laugh at that.

"What kind of friend wants his friend to get electrocuted with him?" I say.

"One that is afraid to die alone. Man, I'd rather die like that then let one of these scumbags stab me," Red replies with a laugh.

"Man, I don't want to get zapped, or stabbed, or killed, for real Red."

"Neither do I. Everything's cool. We have to cook this liquor. You gonna help me or what? The cops don't care, bro."

I nod my head that I'm going to help him. Red's home-made heating element is a disassembled iron. All the plastic has been removed. The only thing left is the steel and an electrical cord. The cord is attached to the wires protruding from the wall. Red drops the disassembled iron into the liquid that he has been brewing for days.

Before long, the liquid begins to boil. A hose is attached to a plastic bag sitting in another bucket—this one filled with ice—to catch the alcohol. The cell looks like a set from a *Mr. Wizard's World* episode.

"The alcohol boils off at a lower temperature than the water content allowing the condensation to filter through the hose and into the bag," Red explains. I listen intently. "The process separates the alcohol from the liquid content creating good old prison moonshine."

The cell is hotter than a summer day in the Arizona desert. Sweat drips from my brow. Ozzy Osbourne's "War Pigs" blares from Red's homemade speaker. Red's cell reminds me of Booper's Uncle Bobby's party room. The party room had old rock n roll posters on the wall, an old table with cigarette scorches burnt into the wood, some chairs, and an old boombox with dried up paint all over it. The party room is where Bobby, his friends, and prostitutes would smoke cocaine base. Occasionally, they would shoot up cocaine, or heroin, in the party room. It was hot, filthy, and filled with lawlessness just like Red's cell.

Again, I am wondering how I got myself into this bullshit. I'm hanging out with Red, making a potion that will surely contribute to some form of violence. Hanging out with Red is simply a way to pass the time in a place filled with boredom.

"What's up with the ice?" I ask.

"That stops the bag from blowing up. If the wires come off that iron it could turn the bucket into a fireball. That's when you better run for real," Red says laughing again.

After two hours of talking and sweating like crazy the process is finished. Both of us are still alive. Red takes a small plastic cup and dips it into the moonshine filled bag. He takes a spoon and puts it on his locker. A little bit of alcohol is put in the spoon, and he lights it on fire. Blue flames dance a tango before our eyes for a minute or two. Red motions me for a high-five.

"Do you know what that means Chad?"

"Nah," I respond.

"It means that shit is gas! These motherfuckers are going to pay top dollar for my liquor," Red says, excitement in his voice.

Alcohol quality is tested by lighting it on fire. The bluer the flame, the longer the dance, the better the quality. I can only imagine what this stuff will do to a person's insides, but that seems to be the least of people's worries around here. Nobody seems too concerned about their insides. Red's liquor sells like hot cakes. The prices vary. For a half pint he pulls in four books of stamps or twenty dollars. A whole pint sells for seven books of stamps, or thirty-five dollars. If you're thirsty, but broke, you can get a small cup for a book and a half. Red caters to everyone.

Within an hour Red pulls in three hundred jail dollars. Not bad for three days of watching a bag of liquid turn into alcohol, then processing it for a few hours in extreme heat. Red shoots four books of stamps in the air toward me. I catch three and fumble the last one. It falls to the ground.

"That's for helping me."

"Four for helping you, and I need four more for the heat, and for your jokes on that wire." I reply.

"I was going to only give you two for being so damn scared." Red says walking out of the door leaving me in his cell.

I know where he is going without him saying. His newly earned stamps will be going to the Sureños. Right now, they own the prison heroin market here at Big Sandy. Many men here are victims of the same addiction. They cannot get out of the infamous cycle of shooting heroin. Black tar heroin through a home-made needle is an escape from prison; it quells the pain of loneliness for a short time.

Drug abuse was the road that led legions of these men through Big Sandy's doors. The addiction is its own journey with no end in sight for the addicted. Like Nokie, the prospect of death does not quench the thirst. With the extreme violence on this end, I will never be able to comprehend why any of these prisoners would ever allow their judgment to be clouded with drugs. It is easy for me to recognize that

I always have to be aware of my surroundings; who's who, what people are doing, and saying. Life could be over in the blink of an eye if I am caught off guard.

Plenty of people will be off guard today, thanks to Red's moonshine. Others will be nodding off into a heroin daze. Danger for everyone—more for those intoxicated. Danger is looming in the distance.

Red is back with a Kool-Aid smile. He knows that the venom he puts in his arm will take him out of here before long, and to his temporary special place. While he cannot escape the razor wire physically, black tar allows him to do so in his mind.

"You don't want to watch me do this shit do you?" Red asks.

"I don't give a fuck." I am interested in knowing how he is going to intravenously contaminate his body. As expected, Red has a home-made device that looks like the needle Jamie Foxx used in the Ray Charles movie. Even prison cannot stop people from dancing with the opiate devil.

Red's prison style syringe is easy to make. It's cobbled from needles stolen from the medical department, smuggled in from cops, visitors, or through the mail. Points for the needles sell for two books of stamps. Once a prisoner has a point, they cut an ink pen in half using dental floss as a saw. The tip of the pen is melted around the needle. Once that's done a bladder is needed. That is usually made from a milk bag's nipple attached to the other end of the pen. All of this is held together by a rubber band.

Prisoners are innovative people. They have to be.

My eyes are focused on Red. The whole situation has me in curiosity's grip.

"Come on man. You got to stare at me bro?" Red asks.

"I just want to see how this shit works, Red."

"You're going to fuck up my high, man."

"Shut the fuck up. Just do what you got to do."

With that Red squeezes the bladder, lighting his veins on fire with pleasure. In a short time, he will no longer be here. His escape is imminent, but he'll be back. He pulls the binky out of his arm and licks the blood spot, bopping his head ironically to Lynyrd Skynyrd's song, "Needle and a Spoon." I watch his eyes grow heavy, as the music plays. His lips curl up into a tired smile. His head nods downwards. After a few seconds he tries to lift his head. His eyes too, but the scenario repeats itself over and over. Red has no control over himself. The poison dances in his veins.

I have seen this dance before. Again, something about this dark place takes me to a sad place from my past.

Looking at Red I see 1993—my father, I have to find him. No one else knows where he is, but I do. When he cannot be found, I know he's in the Party Room. I rush out to find him. He is here—I find him although secretly I hoped he would not be here. But he is sitting in a chair.

"Dad, what the fuck are you doing? You're already high you scumbag. Your son's funeral is an hour away. No one can find you." I say through clenched teeth.

"Come on Chad. Help me."

"Your son just killed himself, and this is what you're doing bitch? Huh bitch?" I yell in anger. The pain of my brother's suicide combined with my anger at my Dad's irrational decisions to be a Dad and not a father causes me to draw my hand back as I shriek. "Fuck you, punk!" And I do it. I slap him across his face. Never would I ever have thought I would have the courage to slap the man who brought me into this world. Today though is the first day that I accept he is nothing more to me than a dope junkie. For all he has put my mother through, the disrespect, the beatings, I think about beating him to death in this Party Room. I'm fourteen. Instead, I spit on him as I leave.

Behind me I hear him say in a low voice, "Fuck you back, mother fucker." He laughs.

I no longer have any feelings for him. Nothing can fix his absence from my brother's funeral, or my life. I run home wearing tears of anger, determined to tell my family I could not find my Dad.

I shake my head as I come out of my daydream. Red getting high took me out of Big Sandy too. I escaped to another dark place—left this one for that one. My eyes focus again. One single teardrop slowly rides down my cheek. I wipe it away swiftly. I focus on Red.

Standing up I say, "You know what Red? You're a fuckin loser. I'm outta here, kid."

Walking out the door of this sauna, I turn back at Red's voice.

"Chad."

"What's up loser?" I respond

"Fuck you back, mother fucker," he says in a slow voice. Then he is laughing uncontrollably.

SEVENTEEN

RUMORS ARE FLOATING. Something bad is going to happen. Sometimes, before a car hits someone, other shot callers get the information. In these situations, they instruct the men in their car to get their affairs in order—take showers, cancel visits, make sure they have food for the impending lock down.

The word is that the Aryan Brotherhood of Texas is going to hit a guy from Texas that is supposedly a snitch. Dinky has chosen the two missiles. One is an Aryan Brotherhood soldier, Billy-Bob, the other is a man named Dewayne from Pennsylvania. Dewayne is not a gang member. When he came to Big Sandy, rumors that he might have checked in at another prison came with him. This is something he vehemently denies. Dewayne linked up with Dinky and his crew somehow. He was given an ultimatum—join Billy-Bob on this mission and "clean his name," or face the wrath of the men he chose to bond with. He has chosen to unleash unprovoked violence on another man to save his own skin.

Cleaning up one's name is something that bewilders me. If a man walks through the doors of Big Sandy after violating the prison rules at another penitentiary, but can clean up his name and in so doing prevent an assault against himself... This contradicts everything I have been told since I been here. In reality, Dwayne is nothing more than a sacrificial lamb that Dinky can cast into oceans of danger to save one of his own gang brothers from the trouble that may come with the planned assault.

Both men have their orders. Armed with prison shanks, shortly after breakfast they head to C-1 housing unit. Unbeknownst to the intended victim, the two perpetrators of the intended assault slip into C-1. Another Aryan Brotherhood of Texas gang member points out the prey as he strolls down the catwalk, his long hair flapping with each step.

Dewayne meets the victim head on. Billy-Bob comes up behind him slashing downward. The tip of his homemade knife punctures his mark's back. As soon as he is hit, the mark dashes towards the officer station. To his dismay the officer is not there. The officer is inaccessible. He is in the unit team area using the bathroom. The mark turns, his back to the office doors. His hands are up now. He positions himself in a boxer's stance. Billy-Bob swings the knife at his target. Red blossoms on the man's white t-shirt. A circle of blood forms on his shoulder, illustrating where he was hit. The target begins to swing wildly. He screams for help. Dewayne swings an empty fist and connects with his prey's head.

The man runs. Both Dewayne, and Billy-Bob give chase. Up the stairs to the second floor, back down, back up. The officer has arrived, alerted by the screams. He too seems to panic. He hits the deuces on his hand-held radio.

Dewayne wraps his arms around the patsy and Billy-Bob closes in. He begins to butcher the victim, stabbing him repeatedly. The screams echo throughout the housing unit. Some prisoners head to their cells. Others look on as if this is just another day at the office. Staff has finally arrived to help the fallen.

Billy-Bob is tackled to the ground. Dewayne's arms are peeled off the wounded man. Both are handcuffed. Prisoners are ordered to their cells. Medical staff arrive with a stretcher to take the long-haired man to the hospital. The prison is locked down only long enough to clean up the blood. Normal operations resume in no time.

Within ten days, Billy-Bob and Dewayne are back on the compound. The sanctions for the beastly assault are a mere ten days in the SHU, a ninety-day loss of commissary and the customary twenty-seven days loss of good conduct time. Not a big deal in this place. Sanctions like this are no more than a joke. There is no deterrent effect for those who entertain the thought of stabbing someone. The consequences for such actions are nil.

A common saying behind these grey walls is, "You have a license to carry a knife, or stab someone, as long as you don't kill them."

Most people are never charged with a new crime unless they kill someone, or assault a staff member. We are the outcasts whose lives mean nothing to society. In prison lingo, "It's all legal around here." Nothing is done to quell the problems here that rack me with fear and anxiety.

For Dewayne, Dinky's word was as good as the person he gave it to. No good. There is a plan in place to hit Dewayne now. I was wrong. They're not going to let him clear his name. The same rumors that I heard about Dewayne must have reached his ears as well. He detoured to the Lieutenant's office on his way to lunch. He asked for protection. Had he stayed, there were men drooling to please Dinky by assaulting him. The PC move stays with you no matter where you go. Once a prisoner checks in, he is doomed. Cleaning one's name is a myth.

With Dewayne gone, Dinky and his crew of misfits lock their eyes on a man in his fifties named Fleetwood. He was an original member of the Texas Aryan Brotherhood gang. The Texas Aryan Brotherhood began as a State prison gang in Texas. This is the way Dinky was introduced to the gang. Many of those gang members later ended up in the federal system where they branched off and formed a new gang which they named, Aryan Brotherhood of Texas. Fleetwood thought he was in a pool of comrades, instead he is in a puddle filled with sharks. Little does he know in just a few short hours he will become shark bait.

This time Dinky dispatches three Aryan Brotherhood of Texas members to draw blood. In the early morning hours, the recreation yard becomes a gladiator pit once again. Staff are oblivious to the three young men in their twenties beating a man who could be their father. Fleetwood is beaten with padlocks attached to belts. He is sitting in the grass, shoes off, his toes curled up towards the bright sun.

A slight breeze caresses the blue grass. The first padlock blow comes from the side. It splits Fleetwood's cheek open—blood like a rushing stream. Somehow he gets to his knees, but that lasts for no more than two seconds. The other two young men swing their weapons. Fleetwood topples over, face first into the dirt. Now comes the hard, black boots to Fleetwood's face, ribs, and back.

I witness this assault from a distance, anger welling up inside me. For a moment, I feel my own desire for violence tease me from within. I forget that the old man is a gang member momentarily. I long for an opportunity to destroy these three, filth-filled men. I envision a baseball bat in my hands, swinging it like Mark McGuire. Rather than connecting with a fast pitch, it's their heads. How anyone can beat up an old man the way they are leaves me both irate, and perplexed. But this is prison; they are gang members. This is not my business so I must suppress my anger along with my craving to intervene.

The assaulters finally tire. They leave Fleetwood laying in the grass, a bloody mess. When the move is called, the aggressors leave the yard making their way back to their housing units. Fleetwood is still laying in the grass like a dead deer when they close the recreation yard.

One officer is tasked with doing a check of the yard to make sure all prisoners are back inside. The officer sees Fleetwood laying on the grass. He calls out, "Hey you! Recall. Time to go inside." No response. "It's time to go, I said," the officer calls out again. He is close enough now to see the blood on Fleetwood's face. "Oh, what the fuck!" he yells out. He's rubbing his forehead as he raises the radio to his mouth with his other hand, wondering how he missed the assault. He mouths something into the radio.

Staff come running out of the doors from all directions. They just stare at Fleetwood when they reach him. They don't know if he is alive or dead. No one checks for a pulse. Medical staff arrive. They move

Fleetwood to the all-familiar stretcher. Somehow, he moans in pain. His face continues to swell from the trauma. I look on in anger, desperate to be released from this land of horrors.

"Lock these mother fuckers down," the captain says. "I'm tired of this bullshit every day. Who the fuck is in that tower?" the captain yells. The rest of us are finally ordered off the yard.

When the door to the cell locks behind me it does not bother me. I feel relieved knowing that we are going to be locked down. Finally, a break from the violence. With the doors locked, I can rest knowing I am safe at least for a few days.

CHAPTER

EIGHTEEN

"WE GOT THE $2,200.00, BOOPER. See if Bouncie will sell us a '62?" I say to Booper.

"Man, he wants $2,400.00."

"Just tell him we got the $2,200.00. We been doing business with him, kid."

"Man, I ain't doing it."

"That's the shit I'm talking about Booper. Your fat ass don't want to do nothing. I'll do it," I say walking out the door.

My breath dances in the cold air as my feet crunch on the hard snow beneath me. The streets are deserted in the frosty night. Streetlights have long been shot out. The City has failed to fix them. This is the land of the undesirables—crack heads, prostitutes, heroin junkies, alcoholics, hustlers, pimps, and nobodies. Who the fuck wants to fix these people's lights? No one. They call this neighborhood Ghost Town after all. If they fix the lights they might have to change the name.

"Hey baby, you trying to do something?" a prostitute appears from nowhere and calls out to me.

"Nah, I'm good."

"Chad is that you?" the voice asks.

I look to the side of the house where the voice came from. The voice belongs to Booper's mother.

"Ya, it's me, and you need to get your ass off these streets Doreen," I say to her.

"Shit, I'm trying to make some money," Doreen responds.

I keep walking towards Bouncie's house, my hand in my pocket making sure my money is safe. If I were to lose that, my drug dealing days would be through. Getting a gun is my first priority.

The steps creak under my weight as I make my way to the door. My knuckles rap on hardwood. I stand there. No answer. I rap on the door, again, louder this time. This time a voice hollers out, "Who the fuck is it?"

"It's C," I respond.

"Who?"

"C *man!* Booper's homeboy"

The door opens a crack. Bouncie looks into my face. "Where is Booper?"

"His fat ass ain't wanna get off the couch, so I came."

"Come in," he says, opening the door for me. It's dark but I see a shotgun by the door, and a pistol in Bouncie's hand. I follow him to the kitchen. The door to the oven is open. Flames dance on the stove. The smell of grease flirts with my senses as the warmth hits my hands.

"What you need?"

"Man, I'm trying to get a deuce?" I say excited.

"Oh? You lil, young, White mutha fuckas done came up. Shoppin' for deuces now?"

"A little something," I respond.

"Man, I'm chargin' twenty-four, but the shit is good. Fiends love it."

"I got twenty-two."

"Can't do it for that."

"That's all we got."

"That ain't all you got! Even young, White mutha fuckas tryin' to get over on the Black man."

I laugh at this. "Come on man. This time let me win, next time I'll pay the twenty-four," I say trying to compromise.

"You see C, you're a hustler. That fat mother fucka you call your partner, he's a fat, lazy piece of shit. I respect your hustle so I'm going to do it. Next time it's twenty-four."

"When I come for the Big Eight though I need it for four," I respond.

"Big Eight? You're moving fast. Take the deuce and do what you do."

I count the money out. Bouncie hands me the deuce. Walking through the snow I think to myself that this partnership thing with Booper might not work out much longer. Like an omen to confirm my thoughts I see his mother again in a driveway. She is on her knees, someone's hands in her hair. The guy's back rests on an old rusty Buick. She found someone that was trying to do something. Now she can get high.

I secure my sixty-two in my hand. I squeeze tight. Two ounces, six grams of cocaine. At the age of fifteen I have already become a product of my environment. Here I come Big Sandy. Here I fucking come.

NINETEEN

FTER THE LOCK DOWN the violence never ceases to exist. The thirst to unleash anger on others pulsates throughout the prison. Staff have allowed a former police chief from Louisiana to walk the compound. That's the talk on the line at least. It is alleged that he found himself on the other side of the law for violating the civil rights of the people he arrested.

Part of the intake process is an interview with a prison's captain. The captain decides if a prisoner is safe to walk the compound. Safe... No one is safe to walk the line on this compound; not me, not other prisoners, not staff. This guy is literally a lone zebra among lions.

Two men from the Aryan Resistance Militia (ARM) volunteer to make the hit on the ex-cop. One of the men is Donnie. Ironically, Donnie is from Massachusetts. He's not in our car because he is an ARM gang member. He has nearly seventeen years in on a twenty-five-year sentence. He emits anger, a roughness that cannot be faked. Like Red, Donnie also has a heroin habit that he fuels with proceeds from his moonshining business. He looks like an old Viking, short, stocky, a long graying goatee. Although a little older looking, Donnie is tough as nails. He could have been a commanding officer in any of the several branches of our military. Instead he is a loyal soldier to a prison gang.

When the beating was over, the ex-cop was still alive—barely. He had to be Mercy Flighted to a hospital after this flagitious whipping where he was kicked in the head numerous times with a hard-plastic tipped boot. Within thirty days, Donnie is out of the SHU, pats on the back for a job well done.

The saga at Big Sandy swirls like an out of control tornado. Gazing out the window, my eyes look past the razor wire to the hills where trees dance slowly in the warm wind. Daydreaming of home, my family, my mother, the people I care for. Tease. No one can know how I really feel unless they've been in this prison. Trapped in a dangerous place, wishing I could take back some of the decisions I made, I wonder how many other men look out their windows craving a second chance at life, silently telling God that if He would only grant their request they would never reoffend.

Big Sandy has a way of making even hardened men appreciate life, liberty, and the pursuit of happiness. The old saying, "Crime doesn't pay," rings true. My most treasured fantasy is being on the other side, climbing the trees that sway in the wind. Running through the tinted, blue-green grass to a hiding place is a fantasy imprinted on my subconscious, amplified by repetition.

A knock at my cell door jolts me from my run in the grass. From the grass back to my cell. I lift my head and nod. Lefty walks in.

"What are you looking at out there?" Lefty asks. He walks to the window to take a look himself.

"The trees, man. The trees," I sigh.

"Man, with your time, fuck the trees. It's just gonna fuck you up looking out there. You have to accept this is your life for now Chad."

"I know, but I like looking out there."

"Do what you want, but my advice is, 'Fuck the trees, fuck the grass, fuck the world,'" Lefty says. He laughs.

"You didn't come in here to tell me about the trees, right? What's up?"

"Oh shit, no um… there are some new guys just come in. One is from Boston. I'm sure he is going to be in your car, so you might want to come meet him."

I follow Lefty and we approach the new guy. Lefty begins the introduction. "This is Chad, the guy I told you about from New York."

The new guy extends his hand to shake mine. "Frank, I'm from the Cape."

"How much time you got?" I ask.

"Twelve years for heroin. And a gun."

Frank is jittery; I can tell he is nervous. Like myself, he rode that long, lonely bus from Atlanta. He listened to the same Big Sandy stories I heard.

"Come on man. We'll go to my cell to talk away from these dudes," I say.

"As soon as we are out of earshot of the other prisoners Frank begins to pelt me with questions. The fear in his eyes is immediate, the anguish in his voice is noticeable.

"Look man," I say to him, "you're going to be alright. I know you're nervous."

"Man, why would they send me to a place like this? I'm only twenty-four years old with twelve years kid." Franks eyes start to water as he tells me this.

"Cause the people in charge are scumbags. They don't care about shit."

"People are getting killed here." Frank says.

"It's not as bad as the stories you heard," I lie to Frank hoping to calm him down. My intentions are simply to help ease Frank's fears until he can adjust to his new circumstances. If he can make it through the first few days, he will be ok. I know the same feelings he is experiencing.

"Dude, I don't want to die in here. These people running this place don't give a fuck about no one, kid." Frank says this with urgency in his voice.

"Look, you too nervous. Are you hot?"

"It's freezing cold in here. I ain't hot."

"Nah man. Hot, like did you snitch on someone in your case? They call that hot in here."

"Fuck no. I'm a petty ass drug dealer that they sent to this slaughterhouse."

"Ok, I'm going to give you some advice that I should not give you. If you're hot you need to get the fuck out of here 'cause they will hurt you. If not, you're good here." I say this to Frank with firmness in my voice so he gets the point.

"Chad, look at me. I'm not hot, or whatever you call it, but I am scared."

"Here is a little secret for you. I was too, a few months ago when I first got here. I am still here, and I ain't been killed. You're going to make it. Just try to calm down."

For some reason I am determined to help Frank make it. I don't want him to take that long walk out of fear. That could ruin his career. He is nervous, fearful. Scared people sometimes take the walk to protective custody for no real reason other than their misplaced fear. People don't understand that making that choice only makes their stay in prison harder.

�✶━✶━✶

THE CALL FOR CHOW echoes throughout the unit. When I reach Frank's cell, he is laying in his bunk staring at the ceiling. He tells me that he does not want to go to chow. He has to be hungry after the trip. My urging him to join me does little. He protests, telling me that he's tired and not hungry. His fear of being here, of meeting more felons, prevents him from eating.

Steve sees me as I enter the chow hall and waves me toward him. "Hey, you got a new guy from Boston over there?" he asks. I can tell he is wondering why the new guy is not with me.

"Yah. His name is Frank. He's from the Cape."

"Oh, yah. Where is he?" Steve asks with a smile.

"He didn't come to chow. Said he wasn't hungry. Wanted to shower and relax."

I can tell Steve is pissed off although he pretends that he isn't. He thinks everyone should worship him. Those who don't should be brutalized. At least, that is what I think Steve thinks. I dislike Steve more and more with every passing day.

Steve tells me to tell Frank to make sure he is at breakfast to meet all of the homeboys. I agree. I wonder if Frank will still be there when I get back to deliver the message from the puppeteer. If you are from New York or Massachusetts, there really is no choice when it comes to the car. You're either riding, or you're getting a plane ticket out of here purchased with force. The car won't necessarily stab you, but Steve will send three or four guys to kick the daylights out of you. Like most things behind these walls, it's better to take the best of the bad options. Joining the car willingly is much easier; to Steve, refusing the car is rejecting your home boys, your brothers. This is a major disrespect. If you have no loyalty to the people from your state—your brothers—then you do not belong here, according to Steve, Adam, and Dennis.

The job of telling Frank this reality has fallen into my lap. This assignment might not be necessary if Frank disappears before I get back. It's hard for me to fathom being loyal to a group of people that you do not know. I am sure Frank will feel the same. In a place like this though, you have to align yourself with someone. No one wants to be alone in this dog eat dog world. Being alone in here is not the wisest choice. Since I've been here no one has declined Steve's smiling offer to join the homeboys' pack of loyalty. The only problem is, one day you are a brother, the next you could easily become a victim.

Frank is still there when I peer through his cell window. Still laying on his bunk, and still staring at his ceiling. I knock, causing Frank to look up at me. I walk in. I don't wait for him to wave me in.

"What's up?" I say.

"Nothing. Just relaxing." Frank replies.

"Look man, the homeboys were mad because you didn't show up to chow. They want to meet you."

"Man, I just want to relax. I don't want to meet these people."

I laugh at this statement knowing this is not an option. I explain to Frank what a car is, how things work in here. When I tell him about Steve, he tells me he thinks Steve is an asshole and a control freak. Again, I look out for Frank telling him to keep those thoughts to himself because if Steve gets wind of talk like that, he will send some people to hurt him. Frank's eyes light up again.

"See this is the shit I was talking about Chad. These dudes want to kill people for some bullshit."

"Well it could happen, but you have to think before you say or do things around here. Protect yourself by making the right choices in here Frank."

"This Steve guy! Man! Who does he think he is? Whitey Bulger from Southie or some shit? Can I just do my own time, stay to myself?"

"You want the truth?" I reply

"Yah actually, I do Chad."

"Well, the truth is, you can't do your own thing. Trust me. You don't want to be alone in here, even if they let you, which they won't. They would have four or five guys kick the shit out of you. After that you'll be in the hole for four or five months. Then you will be on another plane going to another USP, where there will be more Boston and New York guys waiting to tell you that you have no choice. Either you get in the car, or they kick the shit out of you. So, in the end, you can save yourself a whole lot of misery, and ass whippings."

"So, I got no choice is what you're telling me?"

"Listen Frank, this place is like living under a communist government. Steve is at the top of the pecking order. You cannot talk bad about Steve, Adam, Dennis, Ronnie, or the car. Your best bet is to go along with the get along. Stay out of the way, follow the rules, and pray to God your points go down so you can go to a medium security prison."

Frank is getting the message. He nods his head, agreeing with my words. "Do you think I'm going to make it here Chad?"

"As long as you didn't tell on anyone you will."

"I got twelve years. I ain't supposed to be in a USP. I have no idea why they sent me here."

My response is simple. "There are a lot of dirty people out there Frank. No one cares about where they send you. If you live or die, no one gives a shit. Why? Because they go home every night to their family. If a bed is open in Big Sandy when your number comes up that's where you're going kid. This system sucks, and we are swept up in it."

It's near to lock-in time. I shake hands with Frank, and prompt him to try and get some sleep. I tell him to make sure he is up for breakfast in the morning, fulfilling my obligation to Steve. Tonight, will not be an easy night for Frank, but I think he will make it.

As I lay in my bunk, I find that my night, too, is difficult. Mental exhaustion has set in from dealing with Frank. Usually when the lock is in place for the evening, the stress subsides. You can relax to a certain extent then. In here with Mr. Young as my cell mate, I know I am safe. One more day down on my forty-year sentence. Big Sandy has a way of draining its inhabitants—mentally, emotionally, and physically. Only God can hear my cries. My heart aches for just one more chance at life. Just one more chance at freedom. Every rising sun comes with the perplexity of wondering if I can make it through another day. With so little hope of ever being out there again, ever finding true happiness, I fiddle briefly with thoughts of suicide. This is my never-ending nightmare. There is no escape—when the sun rises my daily hurdles transcend limits that seem as though they are impossible to overcome.

CHAPTER

TWENTY

THE U.S. PRISON POPULATION was 1.5 million prisoners at year end 2017, and the population of jail inmates in the U.S. was 745,000 mid-2017. There were 1.3 million prisoners under State jurisdiction and 180,000 under federal jurisdiction. From the end of 2016 to the end of 2017, the number of prisoners under federal jurisdiction dropped by 6,100 (down three percent), while the number of prisoners under State jurisdiction fell by 21,600 (down one percent).

By citizenship status, non-citizens made up roughly the same portion of the U.S. prison population (7.61 percent) as of the total U.S. population (7.0 percent per the U.S. Census Bureau). These numbers are based on prisoners held in the custody of publicly or privately operated State or federal prisons.

The imprisonment rate for sentenced Black males was more than twice the rate for sentenced Hispanic males and almost six times that for sentenced White males. 12,336 per 100,00 Black males compared to 1,054 per 100,000 Hispanic males, and 347 per 100,000 White males. At the end of fiscal year 2017, nearly half of all federal prisoners were serving a sentence for drug trafficking.

While the numbers are falling, many federal prisons are still overcrowded. With overcrowding comes agitation, with agitation violence. Most of the violence is relegated to U.S. Penitentiaries— maximum security prisons like USP Big Sandy—which house mostly high security offenders.

USP Florence located in Colorado saw a massive riot between White and Black prisoners on April 20, 2008. Some white supremacist convicts were celebrating the birthday of Adolf Hitler with prison-made moonshine out on the recreation yard. At some point the White outlaws began yelling racial epithets at Black prisoners. The white supremacists armed themselves with rocks, prison shanks, and other improvised weapons. A battle between both races ensued. It involved over two hundred prisoners and lasted more than thirty minutes.

In an attempt to stop the riot, guards fired more than two hundred M-16 rounds, three hundred pepper balls, ten tear gas canisters, and sting grenades. When the dust settled, two prisoners, Philip Lee Hooker, and Brian Scott Kubik lay dead from gunshot wounds. Over thirty prisoners, and one staff member were also injured in the free for all. Maximum security federal prisons reek with violence. Soon after the riot, Sara Devely, the Warden at Florence, received an Excellence in Prison Management award. One of the biggest problems I see being part of this federal prison system is that there is no accountability. No one cares if prisoners are killed or assaulted.

August 10, 2008, shortly after the riot, another prisoner took a life at the Florence prison.

The violence at Florence also extends to the visiting room. A prisoner took a homemade weapon to the visiting room with him. He cut his wife's neck, then turned his anger toward his mother-in-law. Both left the prison visiting room with superficial wounds, while the warden enjoyed her award.

2008 seemed to be a rocking year for the Federal Bureau of Prisons. On June 28, 2008, prison guard Jose River was stabbed at least twenty-eight times with an eight-inch icepick-like weapon. Two prisoners already serving life sentences were charged with his murder. After a three-month lock down where prisoners were confined to their cells eating bologna sandwiches twice a day they were finally let out of their cells.

With all the pent-up anger, frustration, and hostility it did not take long for more violence to erupt. Over a dozen prisoners were stabbed and the prison was plagued by numerous fights. The prison was placed on lockdown again. In 2017 there were fifty-seven prisoner-on-staff assaults at USP Atwater. These included physical attacks with fists, food trays, and spitting or throwing urine on guards. More than half of those assaults took place in the Special Housing Unit. Not long after Rivera's murder, stab-proof vests were issued to staff. Prisoners like me must find ways to protect our vital organs on our own.

USP Pollock in Louisiana is another prison rife with violence. In April 2007, Tyrone Johnson and Derrick Sparks were both murdered, stabbed with prison shanks. Not only was Pollock the leader in prisoner-on-prisoner murders in 2007, but nothing good ever happens there. A few months after the Johnson and Spark's murders, two more prisoners were stabbed in the stomach. With Thanksgiving right around the corner in November 2007, two more prisoners left this cold world with toe tags on—William Bullock and Donald Till—murdered by other prisoners. Peter Avalos Gutierrez went to meet his maker in January 2008, at the age of fifty-five, after being stabbed to death with a menacing shank.

In Texas, Gabriel N. Rhone was stabbed to death at USP Beaumont—also known as Bloody Beaumont. During the battle, a guard received thirteen puncture wounds. There is a guard-shortage problem in in the Federal Bureau of Prisons.

Wherever maximum-security prisons are, there is also death. The great state of West Virginia is not exempt from prisoner-on-prisoner murders. In April 2018, forty-eight-year-old Ian Thorne was killed during a physical altercation at USP Hazelton. Demario Porter, like Thorne, was killed the same way five months later. This has been going on for years. In February 2015, another prisoner met his fate at the prison when he was stabbed in the stomach. In 2016 prosecutors brought charges against a prisoner after he wrapped his hands around another prisoner's throat and strangled him to death.

USP Hazelton a place known for death and destruction, saw its most famous murder when former Irish Mob Boss James Whitey Bulger was viciously beat to death by at least two younger prisoners at the age of eighty-nine. Bulger had only been at the prison for a matter of hours. He was transferred from another prison in Florida after misconduct with staff allegations. Whitey Bulger was a high-publicity con, known as a snitch. Despite all of this, Whitey was sent to a prison known for murder—the minute he was designated to USP Hazelton, his death warrant was signed. Because Federal Bureau of Prisons staff lack accountability, staff allow prisoners to be led off to gallows of another sort— knives, shanks, steel pipes, fists, and feet. All tools used to send victims to the afterlife. Every day is just another day in the Federal Prison System.

USP Big Sandy, what have you for me?

TWENTY-ONE

"AHHH… STOP… What the fuckkkkk are you doing?"

The screaming reverberates through the vents as I brush my teeth. The wailing is coming from below. It travels through the duct work. I pause momentarily. I am holding the toothbrush in my hand and staring into the mirror. I am intently focused; my attention to the screaming. Anger, depression, fear, anxiety all run through my veins. My life is this. Sometimes I wonder if this is a life at all or a life worth living.

Hearing keys locking doors breaks my train of thought. I continue to brush my teeth. Once again, the officer is yelling the all-familiar, "Lock down." Sneakers squeak across the floor as prisoners scramble; gathering items owed and borrowed, magazines, food, and ice. Everyone seems to want ice when there is a lockdown. Lockdowns seem to be the norm now. Lockdowns are a sanctuary as long as they don't last weeks. Being locked in is a refuge from the day to day violence—the only real escape from the pain.

This lock down only lasts a few hours. Dinky and his misfits were at it again. They decided to hit another White prisoner from the South. He was in the unit below me. According to Dinky, the man had been writing to a prosecutor attempting to cooperate on an unsolved murder. Dinky unveiled this sin claiming he was able to read the imprint on the cover of his victims' writing pad. Simply an excuse made up in his mind. The real reason for his strike was the man had a store, plenty of postage stamps, food, pornography, and books. Dinky wanted all the fruits of his mark's labor. Obtaining these fruits could be achieved through violence. Another sad day for someone on Magic Mountain.

The smell of deep-fried food radiates through the unit making my stomach growl. Someone is making fried food. Like Scoobie looking for a Scoobie snack, I want to find out who is cooking. Is it for sale? Determined to discover the source I follow my nose. As luck would have it, two Sureños who I get along with are deep frying the stuffed flour tortillas they call Chimichangas. I order four with a cold soda. For a split second, I am reminded of the days when I was a small boy enjoying fried food at a carnival. The Chimichangas are filled with cheese, chicken, peppers, and onions—all items stolen from the kitchen. I pay for the food with a book of stamps, thanking them as I leave.

Everyone has a hustle in here. Like Red, the Sureños made a stinger out of wires and stainless steel. They took a hard-plastic garbage can, cut it down with dental floss, and turned it into a deep fryer. People deep fry raw chicken purchased from whoever can steal meat from the kitchen. Convicts who work as butchers have everything for sale—beef, pork, hamburgers, chicken patties, and fish. Regular kitchen workers sell vegetables—fruits, raw rice, pasta, premade sandwiches, oatmeal, and desserts. The three things that people care about in here are food, drugs, and alcohol. The men that are hustling are doing so mostly for one of the three.

Those selling drugs in here at the higher level are doing so not only to live well behind these walls, but also to pay for lawyers. They call these acts Penitentiary Chances. Penitentiary Chances are chances people take selling drugs inside that could result in new criminal charges, or death. In here when you're the man with the drugs and money you become a target of those thirsty for what you have. You have what the vultures want. Overzealous guards, the few who aren't scared, also target the drug dealers. With the drugs comes mountains of problems. The problems are worth the risk when you're chasing freedom.

Two doors down from me another guy sells what people refer to as Spitarettes, or Chewports. Tobacco products are no longer sold in the commissary in federal prison. Many of the guards chew tobacco. They carry empty soda bottles that they spit in, along with the chew that has been in their mouths. When those bottles go into the trash, a few select prisoners with access to the garbage snag the bottles. Like an episode from a scientific show, they set up a lab in their cells. First, they pour the discarded saliva from the chew. Then they place plastic covers over a hot bowl of water where they put the spit, and chew allowing it to dry. Once it is dry, they have what they call black gold. A big pile of chew that they turn into small Spitarettes. Each one sells for a book of stamps. One discarded bottle can fetch anywhere from six to thirty books of stamps. The thought that anyone would smoke anything that came from someone else's mouth makes me want to vomit. Everything is for sale—food, drugs, alcohol, legal advice, pornography, even sex.

We're hanging out in Red's cell—Red, Frank, and me. The music plays loudly as we laugh and joke among ourselves. Frank has been here for over a month, slowing acclimating to his new living arrangements. Dennis, Adam, Steve, and some of the other fellas came over to meet Frank on his second day. He never made it to breakfast that morning, so they showed up in the unit. After that morning, Frank never missed another breakfast.

"Chad, do you think you're ever going to get out of here?" Franks asks me.

"This rathole?" I respond.

"No man. I mean out of prison in general," Frank says, a look of despair on his face.

Rubbing my thumb on my chin, I stall for a moment before I answer. "Praying and hoping 'cause I can't take much more of this shit." Whenever I think about my case, or the situation I'm in, my throat gets dry. I continue, "Listen Frank, I got a phenomenal lawyer from New York handling my appeal. She's Jewish, and Jews are good lawyers."

"Chick lawyers are always smarter than men. Plus, women care about people more, ya know?"

"She works at a law clinic in New York too, so that's a good thing."

"Do you think they respect female lawyers?" Frank asks.

"Jewish chicks named Jillian they do," I say with a laugh, trying to end the conversation about my case.

"You ever see what she looks like?"

"Why? You trying to date my lawyer, jerk off?"

"Come on man. I'm just asking kid."

"Nah, I ain't ever seen her, but she has that New York City accent like Rosie Perez from *White Men Can't Jump*."

Red and Frank laugh. Red says, "That movie sucks, but I hope that Jewish chick gets you out of here Chad."

"That makes at least two of us Red."

"Me too," Frank chimes in. "I want you to get out of here."

Red's country music blares through his homemade speaker.

First thing I remember knowing was a lonesome whistle blowing,
Was a lonesome whistle blowin'
And a young un's dream of growin' up
...
Mama tried...
I turned twenty-one in prison doin' life without parole
No one could steer me right but Mama tried, Mama tried
Mama tried to raise me better, but her pleading, I denied...

With the conversation we are having, I think Merle Haggard's "Mama Tried" is a hell of a tune to be playing. My mother tried too. It was my own decisions that resulted in me being "twenty-four doing forty years without parole." Silently, I pray my attorney can win my appeal. My sanity rests on hope in the success of that appeal.

"That's the deuces bro," Red says. We all stand up and look out the window into the recreation yard. Nothing there. We peer deeper into the yard. The yard is calm. A lake on a warm summer night. Yelling and squeaking sneakers pulls our attention from the window to our unit. When Red opens the door, the noise engulfs us. I see a White prisoner running down the range with blood dripping from his nose. Instantly, I am ready to pounce. Red senses my uncomfortableness. He grabs my shirt.

"That's the White dude, Dog. He's with the Blacks."

I freeze as what Red says registers: he's with the Blacks. The first thing I think is some Black prisoners are attacking a White prisoner. If that were to happen, stalling could cost me or others our lives. In this place you have to meet violence with violence.

Dog is hemmed up by two ARM gang members. He looks like he's been stabbed, but it does not stop him from returning fire with his fists. A heated battle ensues. Dog throws lefts, and rights at a guy named Josh. I cheer inside for him, willing him to win. He moves to the left with the wall covering his back and throws an overhand right. With the agility of a professional fighter, he moves to the right throws a jab, and follows it up with a hard right. A left uppercut next. Josh crashes to the floor, a heap of clothes. A knife tumbles from his hand, clanking, skittering across the concrete floor. Dog is ready to pounce on Josh. His knockout punch appears to have escalated his fury.

Josh's partner disappears momentarily; he reappears with a broom. The first swing misses, Dog weaves away from the strike. The second swing comes fast and hits Dog in the head. As he stumbles back, he shakes his head trying to get his bearings back. Dog's too late. A third swing to the body, the fourth—a crushing blow to his head—sends

Dog to his knees. His eyes lock onto mine, pleading for me to help him. I cannot help him. He made his choice a long time ago. Josh is back on his feet, knife in his hand. The shank strikes Dog in the neck. Blood spills like a broken faucet. His adrenaline enables him to make it to his feet. With one hand on his neck he sprints toward the guard's office. His pursuers give chase. As is custom, the deuces have brought staff flooding into the unit. Dog is able to run through the unlocked door into the arms of those able to save him.

Josh and his partner are ordered on the wall. After a quick pat-frisk they are handcuffed and led out of the unit to the Special Housing Unit. Before the yelling begins, I make my way to my cell. Mr. Young is already there. Before long, I hear the hard steel lock clank behind me. This time I don't feel the regular relief. A piece of me is burning hard. I feel as if a part of me is transforming, taking me to a place where I could hurt Josh and his friend with no remorse. Fire should be met with fire, anger with anger, violence with violence, ruthlessness with ruthlessness. Big Sandy can turn a good heart, black.

I look out the window in my cell door. I see blood everywhere. There is more than I would have thought. Other prisoners are ignoring the call for lockdown. Instead, they are going to the showers and filling garbage bags with ice to keep any perishables cold for as long as they can. Others stop off at the store man's cell. Our store man is a Black man from DC named Bo. Bo sells commissary items from his cell. Everything from cold sodas to chips, cheese, cookies, and meats. The mark up is about thirty-five cents on every dollar.

As I stare out the window at the commotion, I think about Dog. I spoke to him on many occasions. He often talked about his son, and his daughter, and how he was looking forward to getting out of here so he could spend time being a Dad. Dog was a likeable guy in his thirties, serving seven years for weapon's possession. Originally from New Jersey, he relocated to Tennessee. Now he might have lost his life here in Kentucky. While my heart is beginning to darken, there is still a part with kindness. My kindness allows me to hope that Dog makes it, that his life, his hope to be a father, does not end here. If Dog dies, I know this lockdown will not be short.

Watching the attack on Dog made me want to intervene, but there was no way I could. Dog is Irish like me, from New Jersey, but he made a mistake when his feet hit the soil here. He made a choice to ride with the Blacks. Once he did that, he was dead to the White prisoners. He was now considered Black. Whites don't get involved in Black business, and Blacks don't get involved in White business. Dog came to Big Sandy prior to Adam and Steve's arrival. Had he come here after those two showed up, he would have been in our car. In our car the likelihood of two White gang members stabbing him would have been low. Had they done so, we would have come together and massacred both Josh and his partner.

After watching Dog's incident with no Blacks intervening, I am unsure if they knew he was part of their car. Most people assumed that Dog rode with the Blacks. Dog probably liked it that way. Two Black prisoners in our unit usually sit at the same table with Dog in the mess hall. One of them is from New Jersey, the other is from Brooklyn, New York. Neither man came to his aid. Like everyone else they were simply spectators, not participants. I feel a disdain for both prisoners for not intervening, or at least making sure that Dog had a fair shake. Maybe they knew this was going to happen before it took place and were ordered by the shot caller not to get involved.

The prison is locked down. Again. Looking out my cell window I see two other prisoners dressed in white suits that resemble astronaut uniforms. These are the only two convicts out and about in the prison. They are here to clean up the blood. Both are designated to clean up blood and other bodily fluids. There is no shortage of work here at Big Sandy for the men in the moon suits. According to prison standards, this is one of the best jobs to have in large part because it pays well. The assignment pays a little over a hundred dollars a month.

I would never think twice about a job like that. Disease runs rampant among prisoners behind these dark walls. HIV and hepatitis are at the top of the list. That alone makes the blood duty undesirable to me. The hundred dollars lures others in though.

WE ARE ON OUR FOURTH DAY of the lockdown when Mr. Young appears to have a nervous breakdown. It started this morning, shortly after guards shoved paper bag breakfasts into our cell. He was angry that the bags had one apple, two pieces of bread, and a pack of powdered milk. How's a man supposed to survive on that? He could not understand.

When two raggedy bags come in for lunch with more of the same, Mr. Young punches the door. The sound of his fist hitting the hard metal pulls me from the James Patterson book I am reading. Mr. Young's left arm rests at the top of the door. Staring at the back of his head, I hear him weeping. Big Sandy has broken this old man. A Vietnam veteran who saw combat has been shattered by the violence, loneliness, and desperation that engulfs this small area of the Blue Grass State. He stands at the door crying, rambling about his age, and how this whole system is wrong. Both of our brown bags are on the floor.

I can do nothing but lend an ear; listen to his sorrow. My heart hurts to see Mr. Young brought to tears. From Vietnam to federal prison— this is what his life has become.

"I'm sixty-three years old Chad. I should be watching my grandkids grow up," Mr. Young says between sniffles.

With understanding in my voice, I respond, "You're going to be alright Mr. Young. Just hang in there buddy. You'll be home before you know it."

"Chad, there just ain't no real men in this prison. Men make their own decisions. Life decisions. You understand me Chad?" he says through clenched teeth, tears running down his cheeks.

"I can't walk out of this cell if I wanted to and call my family. I can't get myself anything to eat when I am hungry. Do you understand that young man?" I nod in agreement, listening as he speaks.

"I understand Mr. Young. This is a sad life, but we're going to be ok." I say this with some reservations. I want to make him feel better about our current circumstances. His words ring true in my ears. This is a very sad reality that I don't want to accept—we can't even get something to eat if we are hungry— which we are with the brown bags three times a day.

The guards are yelling that its shower time prompting Mr. Young to speak again. "Oh, so nice. It's been four days, and now they want to march us in cuffs to the shower?"

Showers might do him justice, calm his nerves, I hope. I like Mr. Young. I feel bad for him. There is a respect that I have for him like what a grandson might have for his own grandfather. Mr. Young has been in prison for seven years on a fifteen-year sentence for armed bank robbery. He swears up and down that he is not guilty. I believe him.

Most people don't claim to be innocent; they complain about the draconian sentences they received. Federal mandatory minimums have destroyed many lives by sending non-violent offenders to places like this where they are forced to do what they have to do to survive behind this razor wire. Sometimes they are forced to become violent. Without violence they too will be devoured.

Shower time has finally arrived; the simple event brings much relief. Being able to walk out of the cell to stretch your legs brings with it a small amount of joy. Our unit manager, Ms. Chace, is at our door with her secretary, Ms. Hack, to cuff us up for showers. I put my back to the door, squat down and send my hands through the slot to be cuffed. As Ms. Hack cuffs me her soft hands brush my fingers. Her perfume is light, but I can still smell it through the door. A normal person could never fathom how good it feels just to have a woman grab my hands while cuffing my wrist. The saying, "There truly is nothing like a woman's touch," resonates in that small moment. Her Kentucky accent is soothing, her politeness is delightful in such a contaminated place.

This is the first time I have come in direct contact with a woman in many years. Hands cuffed behind me, I grab my towel and soap off the desk. The door opens and Ms. Hack escorts me to the shower.

The hot water streams down my face, caressing my cheeks like a waterfall. Hot water, Mr. Young's breakdown, and the touch of a woman break me down. The smell of Coast soap floods my locked concrete shower. My thoughts go to February 4, 2003—the life I once had.

Snow, pristine, glistening in the light of the moon. I stop at the corner and look to the left. As I turn my head to the right, he's there running towards my truck, gun pointing straight at me. A car is in front of me. I cut the wheel to the left, but I can go nowhere. Another man with a mask and a chrome pistol; he is almost at the driver's side. In my panic I assume I am being robbed. I take a moment to pray they do not kidnap me for a ransom. I am trapped. They got me. And then I see the blue lights as more men jump out of police cars.

The nine-millimeter is pressed to my temple. I see the shiny piece of metal of a Rochester police badge in my peripheral vision. Orders are barked at me as I am ripped from the driver's seat and thrown to the hard, cold pavement. Snowflakes float down from the dark sky. I know it's all over. Booper's long gone. We parted ways when he turned fifteen. I found out he started smoking cocaine base. That was the excuse I used. Like Biggie said, "Blow up like the World Trade Center." Everything was blowing up as I lay in the cold wet snow. The cuffs tighten on my wrist. I wish I were being robbed or kidnapped for a ransom. Anything else would be better than this reality.

My stomach quivers as if I'd just been hit with a left hook to the abdomen by Mike Tyson. I lay there sick and frightened. The cop tells me if I move he'll shoot me in my head. I decide to stay motionless in the snow.

As I rub the Coast into the skin on my face, I begin my own silent weeping. This one thought brings back that whole experience once again. That same left hook to the stomach area hits me again. Just as hard. The only thing that has changed is the date. Everything hurts all over again. The pain is still excruciating.

Sometimes I think of her. Not as much as before, but the fear, frustration, and faithlessness of Big Sandy makes her dance in my mind. At twenty-four, I lost her—a beautiful wife, two little girls, Tiara and Joy, dancing to Michael Jackson's "Thriller"; watching *Lilo & Stitch*, *The Lion King*, *Dora the Explorer*, counting to ten in Spanish. Vivid memories. Jen was her name. Dinner at our favorite restaurant, Pasta Villa. Good conversations, laughs, good times. Life as I knew it; forever gone.

"Your life as you know it may very well be over…" I think that's what the Judge said. It's all a blur now. The salty tears run down my face. I punch the shower wall, hard, over, and over. My eyes burn like hot coals as the emotions run over me. Nothing left but shattered memories, and dreams. No one to blame for the losses but myself—my irrational, and irresponsible decisions.

"Let's go man. You have two minutes. Other people need to shower," a male guard's voice rings out.

Defiantly another prisoner yells, "Fuck you."

"Yeah. Alright," the guard sneers back.

This exchange brings me back to Big Sandy. I try to calm myself. I rinse my face carefully. I'm not going to let anyone see me in this state. This moment of weakness. Not even Mr. Young. Surely not Ms. Hack.

TWENTY-TWO

MR. YOUNG IS IN BETTER SPIRITS. Must have been the hot shower. I climb into my bunk and pick up the book I was reading. Concentrating on the words that fill the page is difficult. Ms. Hack clouds my mind. Mr. Young is staring at me.

"What the hell you thinkin' on up there boy?" he asks, his southern drawl emphasized and molasses slow.

"Ah nothing Mr. Young." I say with a smile forming on my face.

"Nothing my ass," he argues. "What is it?"

I chuckle at Mr. Young's use of profanity. He seldom throws cuss words out of his mouth.

"Ahh I was just thinking about home, and a little about Ms. Hack."

Mr. Young laughs. I feel a little embarrassed admitting I was thinking about the prison secretary.

"Boy, she sure is purty ain't she?" he asks.

"What the hell is purty? Do you mean pretty?"

"Oh hell. Ya know what I mean."

"Well Mr. Young, she is an attractive woman, and her whole demeanor makes her even cuter."

"What are you going to do Chad if you ever get out of here?" Mr.

Young asks, raising on eyebrow.

I look down at him from the top bunk. "I have to get out of here first Mr. Young."

"Yeah, well we all have to get out of here, but if and when you do what are your plans?"

"I have all kinds of plans Mr. Young. A lot of dreams, but at the end of the day I just want to be normal. Have a good job, good woman in my life. I'd like to have a son someday. Coach his football team, take him fishing. All the things we are supposed to do. That's the stuff that would make me happy. Simple things, Mr. Young. Simple things."

"Do you believe in God, Chad?"

"Of course, I do."

"Well you better start praying for a blessing, when the feds get ya can't no lawyer get you out of here. Only person can get you out of ol' Big Sandy is God. I was raised on that Bible, and there are blessings to be had if you work for 'em."

"Oh Mr. Young, I pray for one every day," I respond.

"Did ya like that ol' boy they were jumpin' on the other day? Ahh... Dog Pound or whatever they called him?"

"Ya. He seemed like an alright dude," I responded.

"Well, Ms. Chace said the boy ain't die anow, so he's alright. It looked to me like they stabbed him good. Thought he might have died."

"Yea it looked bad, Mr. Young."

"He's going to live, so that's a good thing. Don't much like seeing people die Chad. Seen plenty of it in Vietnam. Seen some bad things there, and if I don't have that PTSD shit by now, I will when I leave here. Since I have been here, I seen some God-awful things boy. For the life of me, can't understand why these boys in here want to kill each other."

"They're lost Mr. Young. Most of these people are never going home. And if they do, they know they're going to be old. Too old to do anything with their lives. So, life as they know it means nothing—they lash out at other people. I guess it's their way of dealing with their anger, pain, and hopelessness. What do you think about that?" I ask.

"Being you put it like that, I see it. Don't mean I agree with it though."

"Neither do I, but I think it's the truth. These guys have no incentive to do the right thing. Good time is a joke, and the ones who ain't never going home what do they got to lose?"

There is no response when I finish speaking. The hot shower *has* relaxed Mr. Young. I hear him breathing hard. I look over the side of the bed to see him fast asleep.

WITHIN TWO DAYS the lockdown is lifted. The usual hustle and bustle of prison life is back into full swing again. Big Sandy almost left some more children fatherless, this place almost claimed Dog's life. How quickly he's been forgotten around here, but not by me. The violence in this concrete city is shocking.

Mr. Young has learned what really happened with Dog. Quick to share it with me he motions me to our cell. Dog was drinking wine with Josh, and his battle buddy. Someone handed Dog four stamps that they owed Josh and asked Dog to put the stamps in Josh's room. In his drunken stupor Josh accused Dog of pocketing the stamps. Dog claimed he put them in Josh's room. Words were exchanged, and before long fists, knives, and broom sticks were flying. Dog's life hangs in limbo over one dollar.

The end result is Dog wound up in the hospital. Josh and his partner went to the Special Housing Unit. They won't be in there more than a few weeks. They will be back on the compound to wreak more havoc on this place. The prognosis on consequences for violence around here is bleak. The person who will suffer most is Dog. Once released from the hospital, Dog will also be housed in the Special Housing Unit for much longer than the two others. Dog will be in a solitary cell for four or five months, waiting to be transferred to a new prison. For his own safety, Dog cannot come back out to population here.

Stabbing people here is the norm, with little to no consequences for such violence. That makes stabbing practically legal behind the razor wire. In the real world, I imagine morality would prevent a person from lashing out and stabbing another person over one dollar. There is no morality here. Moral turpitude permeates even the lowest levels. It's a new set of rules when the door slams behind you, and the foam smiley face shoes come off.

Dog's new home is not special by any measure. I see nothing special about being locked in a cell for twenty-three to twenty-fours a day. Five days a week, prisoners are allowed to go outside where they are locked in a dog kennel a little bigger than the cells they are living in.

It's non-stop action in Big Sandy's SHU. Keeps the guards busy. The usual action consists of hunger strikes, cell mates fist fighting, stabbing matches sometimes, and staff assaults. Even in the SHU prisoners figure out ways to make vulgar prison shanks.

There is more. One of the most despicable assaults that happens in the SHU is called, "Shitting 'em down." Shitting 'em down is usually reserved for staff. Prisoners will urinate in a container, mix that with feces, and store it for days. When a guard opens the food slot, the prisoner will fling this concoction at their target. This is usually done when a prisoner feels he has been disrespected by a guard. But some men have mental health problems and will shit 'em down for no other reason than a good laugh.

Many of the cops that work in the SHU go out of their way to make things harder on their wards than they already are. Most staff members have a natural dislike, or hatred, toward the men imprisoned here. Guards like to make life miserable for prisoners. They fail to realize that imposing punishment is not part of their job description. Punishment comes from the Court. Guards shouldn't be handing out punishment. Guards throw prisoners' mail, court-approved legal documents, personal photos, and other property in the trash. Guards withhold meals. Guards intentionally skipping a person waiting for his court mandated one hour of fresh air is the norm. These small violations cause prisoners to lash out. Other times guards provoke prisoners into physical altercations, thus justifying five or six cops beating a man into oblivion.

The SHU also has what are called Four Point Cells. Inside the cell there is a bed, fastened in the middle of the floor with latches in four different places. A prisoner is laid on the bed with his left hand handcuffed to the left side of the bed; the right hand finds the same fate. The left ankle is then cuffed to the bottom left side of the bed. The same for the right. When the Federal Bureau of Prisons Four Points a man, they strip him of all dignity. Most times they leave the person naked in that position for hours. Some men cry, others scream for hours, while some hardened men lay there quietly, accept their fate, all the while contemplating their silent revenge.

This is our American system of Justice breaking even the toughest of men.

One hour of outside recreation five days a week is important to a person in the SHU. It is the only form of relief for a person left in extreme conditions. Denying a person this opportunity for no legitimate reason other than being nasty guarantees anger. With anger comes the desire for revenge—men always want to cause pain to the person seen as the oppressor. Chances to seek retribution are far and few between so when opportunity does knock—an open food flap on the door, for instance—shitting 'em down is the usual retaliation.

Cops in the SHU are a renegade breed; they come off as fearless. Some of their bravery comes from the fact that they know the men in the SHU are locked behind steel doors, and when they leave the steel enclosures their hands are cuffed behind their backs.

Most prisoners in the SHU are celled with another prisoner. As most things go around here, Whites are housed with Whites, Blacks with Blacks, Hispanics with Hispanics. Going into a SHU cell can be dangerous if you don't already have a relationship with the convict in the cell. Some prisoners want to be left alone, others have mental health issues, and some are violent just because. If there is already a prisoner in a cell where the guards are placing someone new, guards will open the food flap and handcuff him before opening the cell door. The new prisoner will be put into the cell and then the door closes on both men.

A person walks into the cell without any clue about what kind of weapon the other guy might have. Someone must have the handcuffs undone first. One guy's hands are free, while the other guy is still handcuffed behind his back, defenseless. If the convict in the cell dislikes the new occupant, or simply does not know the guy, sometimes he assaults him. Guards will not open a SHU cell door until they hit the deuces, and other staff respond. Many prisoners have found themselves on the receiving end of a vicious attack, sometimes stabbed, while handcuffed behind their backs.

Figure 9 - Photo of the Special Housing Unit (SHU).

The SHU is a lonely place. Each cell has a toilet, a sink, two metal bunk beds and a shower. Some cells have a desk with a chair. Everything is bolted to the floor to prevent them from being moved or used as weapons. Nothing stops the innovative prisoners from cutting knives out of the steel, sharpening the metal on the concrete floor, and turning the object into a killing machine.

This is Dog's new home after being the victim of an assault over four stamps—one dollar. I doubt Dog stole four stamps from anyone, let alone a gang member. The attack was motivated by some other reason. It was likely Dog's East Coast roots in conjunction with his choice to associate with the Blacks. Most of the White gang members at Big Sandy are from the West Coast. A natural vein of enmity between White, West Coast convicts and East Coast convicts runs deep in the federal system.

Josh and his people must have asked around about Dog's status, and gotten confirmation that he was a loner, and not in the Black car. If they were told he was with the Blacks the assault would not have occurred. There are many unwritten rules behind these dark walls. One is that people do not assault people in other cars, or other races. If Dog was with the Blacks, then he's Black, although his skin is White. Walking the compound, putting on a façade that you're with a car you're not actually with, trying to be a loner, makes you fair game. I suspect this was what Dog was really doing. It made him vulnerable and the prison machine ate him up and spit him out. Once Josh and his cohorts found out Dog's real status, they set out to eat him alive. The four stamps and the accompanying theft allegations were nothing more than an excuse to lash out against a White prisoner who associates with Blacks.

There are plenty of made up reasons to savagely hurt people. USP Big Sandy is riddled with them. When the consequences are no more than two weeks in the SHU for the instigators, men here don't think twice about gruesomely hurting someone else.

The violence behind the razor wire is already wearing me down. Each violent act I observe seems to destroy a small piece of me. The senseless violence here will never cease. It only festers in this environment, fed by sinister convicts trying to escape their own dreams. Trying to escape the demons that landed men behind these walls for grotesque amounts of time—some forever. The free world has written all of us off as animals, barbaric, savages, and deserving of whatever happens to us behind these cold, gloomy, grey walls. We are all human beings, or are we? Have we transformed into savage beasts in a lawless land of misfits? I look into the mirror. A small tear falls from my right eye. I know that Big Sandy is slowing hardening my heart as well.

TWENTY-THREE

A S IS HIS CONTROLLING MANNER, The Viper has ordered another meeting. Everyone in the car has been told to skip dinner and be in the yard on the first recreation move. Something must be brewing in his evil mind. I want to skip the meeting but there is no way I can. Missing any kind of a summons from Steve could send him over the edge. Missing chow pisses me off because it's the first time we are getting real food. The bologna and cheese sandwiches get old quick.

I pass the chow hall, hungrier than a Hebrew slave. The smell of cooked chicken wafts over my senses. Anger engulfs me more and more with each step.

I inhale the warm summer air, taking in my surroundings. I see him in the distance. The Viper is in the east corner of the baseball field. Walking toward him I make a rough mental count of the men that Steve sees as soldiers. He basks in the spotlight of what he sees as his worshipers' attention. My rough count is seventy-three. The numbers are increasing. There are new recruits here, mostly East Coast felons. Some are here looking for protection, others truly worship Steve as their God of Gods— the man who saved their blood from being spilled. I wonder how many really despise the savior. I laugh at the thought, internally.

Curious convicts look on from other parts of the yard as we form a circle around the Viper. The number of combatants in our small prison army shows unity, strength. Steve the vicious Viper has been recruiting new guys from other places—North Carolina, West Virginia, two guys from Texas, and one big fella from Oklahoma. We are labeled Independents. Most of us dislike White gang members for good reasons. For years White gang members oppressed White prisoners who simply wanted to do their own time. Independents have now learned that we have strength in numbers; with numbers we no longer have to be victimized. Most Independents have a desire to rid the prisons we are in of White gang members.

Steve has installed these thoughts in all of us. This way of thinking is part of his sales pitch. His dream of prison prominence intensifies with each waking day. With a hand raised in the air, Steve brings silence over the men. His leadership qualities and his way of grabbing the attention of the heartless felons around him reminds me of President Regan's abilities.

His voice erupts.

"I just want to make sure all of our guys are here. As you can see, our car is getting bigger, and I am pleased with that. We need to all start coming together like this once a week. You know we are all brothers here. There are some new youngsters in our ranks that need to be schooled. Plus, we need to know who everyone is. One of the reasons I called this meeting is cause of these fucking White gang members. I'm fed up with them always trying to oppress their own race and bowing down like cowards to other races. They're running around here talking that White pride shit while buying dope from the jigs. Everyone knows what happened to that kid from Jersey, right?"

Everyone answers, "Yes," in unison, like good kindergarten students listening to their teacher. I see a gun tower window open. The guard inside makes sure we can hear him chamber a live round in his rifle. Just a little notice that if things get out of control, he's there locked and loaded. Steve continues with his lecture.

"Obviously, he was with the Blacks. He was here before we got here but we gave him the option to ride with us, to come back home. He made his choice, and everyone sees what that choice got him. None of his so-called people helped him. That is why you men need to know that what we got here is a brotherhood. Each one of us are our brother's keeper. We have to have each other's back twenty-four-seven." People nod their heads, dazzled by Steve's words.

The Viper continues, "Is there anyone here who really does not want to be part of this car? If so, speak up now. You can walk away with no repercussions."

I almost raise my hand, but the no repercussions thing is a lie. There is no honor among thieves. In here your word is only as good as the person you give it to. If you leave the car, you're turning your back on your brothers meaning your blood is worthless to this group. Just reminded, as they are, about what happened to Dog, who would leave now?

"I talked to Adam, Dennis, and Ronnie about this. No objections from them. You can walk away, be on your own." Steve pauses, giving us all time to think. "On your own you can become a victim to these White gang bitches, or have the niggers rape you." Steve says this sarcastically, but he delivers the message. We understand the meaning.

I keep my hand at my side like everyone else. No one jumps at the offer to walk away from the car. Everyone in the circle is likely thinking the same as I. Those thoughts are of Dog, and his desperation as he looked around for help that never came. I consider the possibilities—the Blacks trying to extort me or any of the many other things that lurk in Big Sandy's dark waters when you're alone. I am convinced once again that the car is my only option. Walking away could be detrimental to my health. 1 stay silent, choosing what I think is the better of the two evils.

There is a food chain in prison. Those alone are at the bottom waiting to be eaten alive. And there are many bottom feeders housed in here, the lowest of the low, looking to scrounge from whomever, whenever, and wherever. Some will take by force, some by fear, or manipulation, while others will take by stealing without the victim knowing who the predator is.

Steve's words—being raped by the Blacks—are used to instill fear. A manipulative tool at his disposal. Rape happens but not too often. Homosexuals are a dime a dozen around here. If any Blacks raped a White prisoner, it would be a transgression so severe it would set off an explosive firestorm of violence. When it comes to raping someone from another race, physical violence is not a possibility, it is a requirement, all repercussions to the wind. Rape would turn into death for the perpetrator. The rapist would be the target of many. Someone would get him. The rape comments were simply to shake up the new guys, to cement their commitment to the car. If they want protection, they need to become the protector. Strength in numbers prevents rape.

The Viper raises his hand, quieting the masses and grabbing the stage once again.

"I'm done with it! I'm ready to get rid of these gang members. I haven't called the shot yet for the sake of all of you, but I ain't taking much more of what they are putting on us, so everyone needs to be on point, ready for battle. If you get the word, 'We got a baseball game. Bring your cleats,' that means it's going down. Be here suited, booted, and bring your knives. We will meet right here. I don't want none of you brothers alone. Find someone in the car that's in your unit so you can hold each other down. We are getting on the battle buddy system. Be with that bro all the time. Hanging out, going to chow, the shower, yard, wherever. When you go to the shower have a point man."

Adam chimes in. "I hope everyone can see, and feel, the friction between us and them scumbags. There is animosity. They are watching us; they are worried we got our numbers up. Don't think for a minute that they won't try to make a move on any one of us. Stay safe. And be careful men."

We say our goodbyes, shaking hands when the rally comes to a close. Hunger swells in my stomach. I reflect on Steve's specific instructions not to be caught alone. Maybe his own paranoia is causing him to overreact, but in this environment anything is possible and no one wants to get caught slipping. Scared people do unimaginable things. Scared people want to leave someone else's blood on the razor wire, rather than having theirs dripping from it.

There are only forty White gang members here. The Boston-New York car has a little over seventy. Other, small, independent, White cars despise White gang members as much as our car does. The Ohio independents have about twenty guys in their ride. Their shot caller is a man serving nearly three hundred years for armed bank robbery. Almost every Independent White car hates White gang members. If we went to war with the gang members, other cars would join in the disposal of them, including Ace's.

The Independent movement has gained traction amongst White prisoners in the federal system. It was borne out of years of gang members oppressing White cons who had no backing, no help. White prisoners were forced to fold to White gang members demands. Those demands came in many forms—money, commissary, family forced to visit and bring narcotics into prison. Being told they were not allowed to change television channels, being moved from cell to cell, being forced to live with less desirable prisoners. Many times knives would be cut out of their beds and lockers. When guards discover these alterations the White non-gang members faced the consequences. Oppression at its best in this unforgiving prison world. Oppression at the hands of those who claimed to love their own people and wanted to lift up their race.

The DWB gang has always been one of the most brutal oppressors. DWB stands for Dirty White Boys. The name says it all. When a gang's name starts with the word dirty, everything that comes after is pollution. Some prisoners have family with money in the real world, others have their own money and people in the real world controlling it. In a maximum-security federal prison, any prisoner with significant financial resources might as well have an X marked on his back. He is an instant target. Gang members will key in on a prisoner like this.

They are easy to spot since they always go to commissary, have nice things, and usually receive lots of mail and visits.

Once they determine a mark has money, a plan is devised to extort the unsuspecting victim. The older a potential victim the better. Older man scare easier especially when they're new to the prison system. Someone like Mr. Young would have been a perfect victim. His lack of money is the only thing that saved him. White gangs plan these exercises in extortion to the nth detail. Everything is always carefully laid out.

It could start with a gang member bumping the target at the microwave, followed by, "Watch where the fuck you're walking old man." That same guy might cut in front of the target at the washing machine, or in the chow line. He might ask the old man, "What the fuck is your problem?" This is all part of the intimidation, all part of the groundwork.

Afterwards two other White prisoners might pay the old man's cell a visit. Heavily tattooed, imposing looking creatures are usually chosen for this part. They inform the prey that the guy who has been bumping into him and disrespecting him does not like him and wants permission to hurt the old man. This is when all the prison movies, the stories the mark has heard, start to manifest into reality. The old man has become the star of the show. Two protectors have showed up in the nick of time to save him, just like in the movies. The two tattooed cons promise to keep the mark safe from the disrespectful maggot pestering him. All of his problems, worries, and fears will disappear in exchange for a small, shall we say, stipend, every month.

The initial fee might be two thousand dollars. Three hundred dollars every month thereafter. It is always explained that one is better off paying rather than checking in or dying. To the victims, it always seems like paying the money is the easiest option. Once a mark pays, the gang swings the door open all the way. The victim has exposed his hand. They recognize his fear. He will live a miserable existence at the hands of guys his children's age. The people who should be looking out for him have placed him in a mental version of a WWE cage match. John

Cena has delivered an Attitude Adjustment. These two pieces of filth may stop by the old fella's cell for a candy bar, or a soda whenever they feel hungry. They might want other small things—rice, sausages, some beans, anything to sate their hunger.

The person who got this all started is part of the same gang as the protectors. He leaves the victim alone. No more problems from him, but the victim's problems have escalated. This was all part of the plan. All three participants reap the continuing benefits of their extortionate scheme. These people never have enough. The prison wheel grinds slowly forward. Before the victim knows it, the oppressors are in his cell again. This time to renegotiate their contract. As if the economy has called for higher payments.

Stress, anger, and anxiety are only a few of the emotions that describe what a person experiences under these circumstances. This was not supposed to be a part of his sentence. He did not ask for this. His only fault: age and financial resources. The hyenas will move in and devour him slowly, piece by piece. The same thing happens on the African plains. All wounded gazelles suffer the same fate. Dirty White Boys in every sense of filth.

This is one of the reasons the Independent movement formed within this concrete jungle. Now it's gaining power. Hatred for all White gang members has slowly begun to form in me as well. It has only taken months for my anger toward them to come to a boil. As Independents, often we stop gang members from preying on innocent victims. This creates friction between us and them. An explosion is destined to happen; the ingredients are being mixed in the kettle. A violent clash is imminent, the only question is when. Secretly I cannot wait. I too have pent up anger that I want to unleash on those I think deserve it.

Prison politics embrace neither mercy, nor compassion. There are only three responses to an extortion attempt: checking in, fighting back, or paying the cost. In the moment, fear causes people to take the easiest available option. In prison, rash decisions tend to be the wrong ones in the long run. Regardless of his age when the first bump comes at the microwave the old man should swing at the bully. Cops will respond, the fight will be broken up, and the old man will go to the SHU pending transfer to another prison. With the all-important *good* detention order.

A detention order is a sheet of paper explaining why a person is being housed in the SHU. If a person checks in (seeks protective custody) the paper outlines that. If it is for a fight, or investigation, the protective order outlines that as well. This single piece of paper can either be one's saving grace or one's doom. When a person is transferred to another prison, other prisoners will demand to see the detention order. If it says the wrong thing the prisoner will be assaulted on the spot, and the SHU will be his home for years. He'll go from prison to prison. With a good detention order for fighting back, a prisoner paves his own way. The extortion attempt will likely be the last one he experiences.

Gang members know how to apply pressure, and who to apply it to. Most people want easy prey. A person who fights back is a problem. Extracting money from a person who fights back never happens. Everyone loses, including the gang members, if they push the wrong person into the corner.

We outnumber the White gang members, and I am looking forward to the eruption between us and them. Backing them into a corner gives me a small sense of joy. My heart hardens more and more especially toward them. Secretly, I like the hardening.

TWENTY-FOUR

IN HERE SPORTS is one of my only stress relievers. Softball season is about to start and our shot caller, the Viper, is starting a team. Most people enjoy softball—playing or watching. I quickly learn that softball is Big Sandy's favorite pastime. But even softball comes with violence, contaminating my one escape from here.

Although the team is being made up of guys from the car, Steve wants to name the team the Boston Red Sox. As a Yankees fan it is hard to play for a team with that name. I'd prefer to play on another team but once again Steve would never allow it. Because I'm already in the car, and a good ball player, I have no choice. Steve enjoys the game, and not wanting to play for him could get me beat off the yard. The way he would spin it is that I turned my back on my brothers. I am now part of the Viper's Red Sox organization.

Softball is a way to get outside of the razor wire. It gives me something to look forward to in a place where meaning is hard to come by. For most men in prison sports is an outlet, whether softball, basketball, football, or handball. Playing occupies your mind. When you're involved in an athletic contest, competing against others, you're focused on the game not on prison politics. You find yourself somewhere else. You might be behind Yankee Stadium playing handball, or at a high school football game back in Texas, perhaps at a basketball game on a court in Baltimore. You're anywhere but here, anywhere but Big Sandy. A man's worries and troubles are gone for the moment, mentally erased for that short period of time. It only lasts for as long as the game goes on, but it is a break from the internal mental struggle that comes with each waking day in prison.

Steve is the pitcher. I am on second base. Our short stop is Luke—the best short stop in the prison. Ronnie Wilson from Lowell, Massachusetts is on third. Adam has left field. When the other pieces are mixed in, we look like the team to beat.

Ronnie comes off as a real tough guy. Like Steve, Adam, and Dennis he came here from USP Beaumont in Texas. Beaumont is nicknamed "Bloody Beaumont" by both staff and prisoners. Because of the violence, USP Beaumont was closed for some time. All the prisoners were transferred to other prisons. Many were sent here. Some say Beaumont makes Big Sandy look like child's play. If Beaumont was worse than this place, I am thankful I never made it there.

United States Penitentiaries or USPs are designated for the worst of the worst. They are mostly designated for the worst men that society has to offer; the most violent, the most ready for mayhem. These prisons are holding centers for society's undesirables, and I find myself here. I am one of our castaways simply because I exercised my constitutional right to trial. The prosecutor offered a plea offer that could have resulted in a ten-year term which would have sent me to a lower security prison, a Federal Correctional Institution. Because I didn't accept the plea offer, our criminal justice system sent me to a United States Penitentiary. That has nothing to do with either correction or rehabilitation. Every breath of fresh air here could be my last. I have known this since day one. My reality and every other prisoners' as well.

Federal Correctional Institutions or FCIs have less violence, and prisoners are rarely stabbed or killed in those facilities. While my goal is to get out of prison, the more realistic goal is to make it to an FCI. Whether I will make it is anyone's guess. For now, I am here with the lions.

It does not take long before the one thing I actually find a moment of happiness in begins to crumble. Just like crackers in a fat man's hand over a hot bowl of soup, our softball team is turning into dust. With their two strong personalities Steve and Ronnie begin to clash on the diamond. Ronnie is from a city in Massachusetts that is home to one of the best Irish fighters to ever get in the ring–Irish Mickey Ward. The poverty-stricken city breeds tough guys. Steve is his own tough guy. Mixing the two is like mixing water and oil.

Steve is the first to quit the team. Adam follows. Ronnie abandons the team shortly thereafter. We no longer have a team. With its demise, my joy is gone. All we have left is a skeleton of a team. Missing key players, we go from a team to beat, to a team that cannot win. Once Steve quit the team, he showed me his true character. Steve's a quitter. More and more I can see through his façade. Occasionally something will happen in life that will change one's opinion of someone in an irrevocable way. When that happens, it shatters the idea someone has built up around that person. If the Viper cannot handle the operations of a prison softball team without quitting, then how can he run the car, or send young men into a prison battle? Maybe he is not a Viper at all. Perhaps he is nothing more than a small garter snake.

Today I am forced to see Steve for the person he is, the fallible human he has always been. No longer the Viper to me, he is simply an egotistic maniac serving life, bent on controlling everyone and everything he can until he is found out. Until other people see what I see, he will remain our shot caller. Any respect I had for him is gone. Steve is a master manipulator, good with words and stories of his life experiences. These stories captivate people, draw them in, and give Steve followers. And with followers, power. That power enables Steve to be the shot caller. So many of these men need a leader because they cannot think for themselves. In this dangerous place, Steve is the comforter for so many. Falling under the spell is easy. I did it just like the rest of the men in the car did.

Our new Red Sox team is 1-5. We have become fodder for the prison's hecklers. Although we are not good, I see the team as a plus because it takes me out of prison and gives me and some of the others a small piece of fun. Anything good in Big Sandy rarely lasts long. Like most things here baseball season will shatter like a plate glass window colliding with a boulder.

It's a warm Saturday afternoon. The sun is shining. A cool breeze blows through the yard. It's the fifth inning and by some miracle we are winning. The batter hits a pop fly out to the outfield right behind our short stop. Luke backs up and makes the catch. He raises his hands in triumph, a form of bravado as if he just won the World Series. During Luke's performance the guy on third base tags up, running home to score a run for the Mexican team.

"Good catch Luke but why don't you fucking pay attention? The guy at third just ran home," I snarl.

Luke doesn't like being scolded. He replies, "Man, suck me."

"What did you just fuckin say?" I ask, giving Luke a chance to retract his statement. All eyes are on me and Luke. Everyone knows he just committed a prison sin by inviting me to suck him. We are walking towards each other. My fury starts to rise. My glove comes off.

Luke removes his sunglasses. In a nonchalant matter he says, "I said you, and everyone else on this field that don't like it can suck my…"

I do not let him finish the sentence. I hit him with an overhand right, followed by a left, and another right. A hook to the temple finishes him. Luke falls to the sand, covering his nose with his hand. His pride devastated, he gets to his feet slowly. Blood falls from his nose to the sand. He knows he just broke two separate cardinal prison rules. For his violation, his nose is broken. You never invite anyone to your midsection. Not in here. Never another race.

The opposing team was filled with Mexicans. I'm not the only person Luke's words invited his love muscle. He invited them as well. Had I not handled it immediately, this could have easily caused a bigger issue. A guard manning the yard stares directly at us. It is a given we are heading to the SHU. The cop calls us to the fence to inquire.

"The softball hit you in the face correct?" He's giving us a chance for some reason.

Luke stands there with an expression on his face that says, you just seen that guy hit me. Why are you asking me that? Get me out of here.

Nabs, another guy in the car, speaks up. "Of course the baseball hit him. He's ok! Right Luke?" He says this as he slaps Luke on the back. It's like they're old pals.

"Yeah. The ball jumped up and hit me," Luke says, while covering his face with his bloody t-shirt.

"Do you need to see medical?" the guard asks.

Nab answers for Luke. "No, he's alright CO. He's a big boy. We got 'im." Nab puts his arm around Luke and guides him out of the guard's earshot. "Listen you stupid motha fucka. You're gonna apologize to those Mexicans, and the guys on the team, or you're getting butchered out here. You piece of shit. You're gonna be the dick sucka, and when you're done you and I tough guy, we're going to see Steve and Adam so they can deal with you."

Nabs' stern Rhode Island accent scares Luke.

Nabs has been in for six years on a fifteen-year bit. Both of his parents have passed away since his arrest. When they died some people said he went crazy—drug use, alcohol, and violence. Nabs has no problem stabbing another man without hesitation. He is known for this. He always has a knife on him. These are not idle threats. Like a scolded schoolboy, Luke apologizes to everyone for his disrespect. His own words could have killed him. In the penitentiary people are always looking for a reason to send things spiraling out of control. These may seem like small things to those in the free world. This unforgiving world twists them and makes them big. Angry men tend to make up reasons to unleash their pent-up anguish, to vent on other prisoners.

My first physical confrontation brings me new respect. Violence is the one thing everyone respects in this dungeon. When people recognize that you are a person who will inflict, or resort to, violence other convicts respect you. Fighting is rarely a fair endeavor at Big Sandy. Today I was able to put on a little show, demonstrate that I am good with my hands. I was an accomplished amateur boxer growing up. Using my hands comes naturally to me. But knowing how to fight well could turn out to be a problem. If people fear you, they will not hesitate to use a weapon or to send five guys at once to attack you. Putting my fighting skills on display may or may not be a good thing. Time will tell. Letting Luke's transgressions go unanswered would have been worse though. It would have left me looking like a punk, a coward. Under those circumstances, I would have been the one answering to Steve and Adam. Expressions of cowardice aren't tolerated. That would have been my one-way ticket to the SHU after a savage beating.

As expected, Steve is unhappy with Luke's actions. This issue causes others to remember that there was a previous issue where Steve got drunk and invited another guy to his groin. He was slapped around for that offense although what Adam had wanted to do was throw him over the upstairs railing. Instead, he was given a pass and a warning to watch how he spoke to people in the future. What really saved Luke was that he's a gunsmith, and thus valuable to the car. He was the car's primary knife maker when the car's arsenal had to be boosted. Luke would spend countless hours scraping lines in the steel beds with stainless steel tools and cutting knives out of the beds. Luke would then sharpen the metal into fine points. In prison, knife making is a long, tedious process that most don't want to undertake. Luke would do this task for hours, never growing tired. Now that the car's weapons stockpile is sufficient, Luke is expendable.

Figure 10 - More prison shanks.

According to Steve, the broken nose is not adequate punishment. Steve wants Luke stabbed for his second violation. Other guys in the car who like him advocate on Luke's behalf. They call for a beating that results in him leaving the yard. To appease the soldiers, Steve reluctantly agrees to the beating. After all, Luke had two strikes not three. But Luke's out all the same. Two missiles are selected. One is a younger guy from Pennsylvania named Bolts. The other is called I.D. Neither man objects to the order to assault Luke. This brings a smile to Steve's wicked face. He basks in those who never object to his directions. In a sick way, I think it excites him that he has this manipulating power.

The hit happens that night. Luke is sitting at the table when Bolts sneaks up on him, a lioness in tall African grass. Leather gloves on, Bolts swings wildly from the side. Luke does not fall, but he is stunned. I.D. strikes from the other side. Luke screams out in agony and falls to the floor gaining the guard's attention. I watch from atop the steps as both men kick and punch their helpless victim. The attack continues until more staff arrive to separate the missiles from their target.

Luke is lifted off of the floor, beat up, bloody, and likely relieved to be getting a transfer far away from this car, this place of despair. If that is all it takes to get away from Steve, maybe I should volunteer for a good beating. A ridiculous thought, maybe, but desperate men think of desperate measures. I cannot fathom any other place being worse than this. There's nowhere that's more volatile than Big Sandy. Maybe I should take the change. Maybe this isn't a bad idea.

Bolts and I.D. are both cuffed up. They look up at Steve for praise. He stands at his cell door like a proud father. Bolts looks at me nodding his shiny bald head as if he's telling me I owe him now. If he thinks that he is sadly mistaken. People like Bolts and I.D. are always trying to prove their worth to Steve. They come in all shapes and sizes. Little do they realize that Steve couldn't care less about them. He has his own agenda. Using these slugs to achieve his agenda is just part of the plan.

TWENTY-FIVE

I AM BEGINNING TO FEEL like a desperate fowl caught in a hunter's trap. I am starting to dislike the guys in the car. I dislike Steve more each day. I dislike him the most. Seeing through his manipulation game gets easier when I pay attention to his actions, the decisions he makes, the way he talks to people. All of these paint a different picture. I was never a follower in the free world. When Adam and Dennis first approached me, I felt I had no choice except to buy into the car's ideology and objectives. Everything they sold me about the car—the brotherhood—is turning out to be a farce.

Time has a way of revealing things. Most of the guys in the car are simply along for the ride. They were fed the same stories I was. Fear made most of us join the car. Big Sandy leaves men in a damned if you do, damned if you don't sort of position. Steve has a way of making people feel like they are indebted to him for being so kind as to allow us into the fold. As a result, when Steve makes a request, no matter what it is, people jump to attention to please the master puppeteer. Assaulting people, making weapons, carrying them to the yard, giving him money, transporting contraband; when he beckons men answer.

I decide not to be one of Steve's do-boys for too long. Frank feels the same way. It's how he's felt since his first day on the compound. Our pockets are empty, so Frank suggests we find a prison hustle. We juggle ideas back and forth but ultimately we decide that moonshining is the only real option we have.

Red introduced me to the lucrative business of prison intoxicants, now Frank wants me to be his partner. Before long, I am smuggling hundreds of Sweet'N Low packets out of the kitchen. I was agitated when Steve had me doing it for him for free; now that it benefits me, I have no problem with it.

Business kicks off with us cutting up potatoes, opening hundreds of Sweet'N Low sachets, and mixing everything together in a bag. Frank agrees to hide the first batch in his locker. I'll take the next one. In four days, we turn water into wine, much like Jesus. I suspect the Lord's process was a little different than ours. We put our makeshift lab together. A few hours later we have home-made vodka. We both take a small sip of our prison potion.

"Damn," I say coughing into my hand. "Who the hell has the balls to drink this shit?"

"Oh, you'll see who has the balls to drink it in a minute or two," Frank says, rubbing his hands together like an excited child.

We put a small amount of our concoction on a spoon, turn out the lights and put fire to it. A blue flame dances in the spoon. Like a gypsy belly dancer, the dance is reflected in our eyes.

"That's gas Chad! We got gas, and with gas we got cash."

Gas is prison slang for high quality alcohol. People are always looking for gas. Gas can chase their sorrows away. We fill eight empty peanut butter jars. I do the math in my head—eight bottles, at eight books a piece, we have three hundred and twenty dollars in jailhouse money. We get a hundred and sixty a piece. Word spreads that the two White boys have some serious rocket-fuel for sale. On a Friday evening it takes all of twenty minutes to sell out. We timed things so we had our juice ready for the start of the weekend. Even in prison, weekend is party time. Frank and I have our own version of Grey Goose. With our first success, our business relationship is cemented. We head to the local hangout, Red's room, where he is tattooing Sad Boy, the Sureños gang member I played handball with when I first arrived. He sips his peanut butter jar of prison vodka as the needle drills into his skin. Sad Boy has his sidekick, Droopy, with him, his own jar in hand. Even though we are different races, and in different cars, the five of us have become close. If anything happened with the Blacks, our car would join forces with the Mexicans. Feeling good off the moonshine, Sad Boy starts imitating Steve. It's uncanny. He's doing it almost perfectly.

"Chad, Frank, I need both of ya to start wearing your boots to chow so you can hide Sweet'N Low in 'em for me. Don't forget the gang members have to go." Sad Boy says this in a fake Boston accent missing as many r's as he can. He knows we disdain Steve. Red pulls the needle from Sad Boy's arm and doubles over laughing. Frank and I are in tears. Droopy joins in. He's playing Dennis.

Steve is bald-headed, skinny, no eyebrows or facial hair. When he talks, he sounds like he just sucked a helium filled balloon down his throat. This guy is my leader? What an idiot I am. This thought in conjunction with Sad Boy's jokes send me into hysterical laughter. For the first time in a long time, I am laughing so hard I begin to cry. Grateful that the small jokes take me out of prison.

The gang that Sad Boy belongs to, the Sureños, is the most serious gang in federal prison in my view. They demand respect, and have no problem turning to extreme violence at the drop of a hat to achieve their goals. Sureños have each other's back no matter the situation or who the problem is with. It doesn't matter if it's another prisoner, a guard, or even the Warden. They will attack like a pack of wild dogs if ordered to do so by their shot caller. The shot caller is usually a Black Hand. Black Hands are the men who run the Mexican Mafia, who in turn run the Sureños. The Sureños have a lot of rules. One of their rules is that they are not allowed to do business with Blacks. Sad Boy was accused of drinking with a Black prisoner while at an FCI in Texas. He says the accusations were false, but it resulted in him being beaten off the yard.

The concomitant security level increase landed him at Big Sandy. Droopy had his own problems at another FCI. He has a penchant for heroin so if I had to guess, his transfer to the Bluegrass State likely stems from his opium addiction.

Droopy is a fearless felon. Two or three times a week he sneaks into the lieutenant's office where staff members keep their personal items. The office door is never locked almost inviting Droopy to stop by. He usually leaves with a pack of cigarettes, or a can of chewing tobacco to pay for his growing heroin habit. Droopy's petty larceny does not persuade staff to stop leaving their things laying around. If they continue to leave their things laying around, they will continue to find their way into the hands of this wonderful magician. Today he is eating a crab salad with his alcohol. Knowing crab salad is not on the commissary I ask, "Where did you get that?"

"Oh, check it out Homes. I got hungry so I stopped by the lieutenant's office and grabbed it out the fridge. I seen it there. Thought they left it for me." He sticks his tongue out as he laughs. Again, I find myself crying from the laughter along with everyone else.

"Man, I ain't never going to get this tattoo done with you crazy mother fuckers in here," Red says when he can catch a breath.

They say there is a fool born every day, and every time Droopy strikes the lieutenant's office the saying is manifested.

The fire alarm startles us, breaking up our laughter. No one seems to know what is going on. This is the first time any of us ever heard a fire alarm go off in prison. Droopy leaves the room to investigate.

When he returns Sad Boy asks, "What the fuck are they doing? Are we in elementary school doing fire drills now?"

"Nah, Homes. They said that dumb ass, White, Crip, kid hit the fire alarm on accident," Droopy replies.

"Who Spivey?" I ask.

"Yah, that's him."

"Everyone outside! Let's go men! Fire in the building. Everyone out." Staff are in the unit ushering us outside. Panic strikes the dorm. Men scramble to hide knives, and other contraband. More staff are swarming the unit ushering all of us into lines so we can be patted down for shanks, drugs, cellphones, or other contraband.

A Puerto Rican guy named Vic from New York, who I have become friends with is caught wrapping a menacing looking knife into clothes on his way to hide it in the washing machine. Vic has a lot of influence in here. Two guards cuff him up. The look on his face is worse than a wild bull at a rodeo. As Vic walks past me in cuffs, he comments, "That dumb ass White boy just fucked up my close to home transfer." I know that he is talking about Spivey. It won't be long before everyone knows he is the culprit.

Once we are all searched, we are led outside. Staff rips every cell apart. Garbage bags filled with wine are carted out of the unit, paraded for all to see. Cells where weapons are found get locked while the people housed in them are located, cuffed, and escorted to the SHU. This was an unexpected shakedown. No one was prepared. Men are upset that they lost knives, and contraband; blood is the only way to pay for the wrongs. As if blood fixes the problem.

SPIVEY LOOKS LIKE a deer caught in headlights when he hears a DC prisoner call out, "Who da stupid mother fucker pulled the fire alarm?"

For a long moment, no one responds. I stare at Spivey wondering what he is going to do. After another long moment we hear his voice. "I did the shit on accident."

"What!? Accident?"

Spivey's eyes widen as he swallows. "It was an accident, bro."

"Accident? You got everyone fucked up, slim."

"I said, my bad bro. The shit was not intentional."

Before long, the DC prisoners are talking with the Crips. The shot caller for Spivey's gang lives in our unit. After the DC prisoners are done talking to the Crip's leader, Spivey gets summoned over to their area. Every car is responsible for their own people. Each car is given an opportunity to discipline those who violate convict rules. Through his own ignorance Spivey has violated prison rules. To prevent things from escalating, his own people have to deal with him. Small things can go from zero to one hundred in a matter of seconds. White prisoners in Black gangs are easy marks when they transgress or break rules. In most cases, Black gang members don't really want a White person in their gang so when he does violate prison conduct, hurting him comes easy. The cries for Spivey's blood ensure his imminent assault.

Prison politics have dictated Spivey's fate. The sole atonement for his transgressions is the shedding of his blood, as if we are stuck in Old Testament times. All eyes are on Spivey. He knows what's in store. Despite the fact that violence is waiting to greet him he is courageous. He does not take the walk of shame. Not checking in could cost him his life. He chooses to gamble. Most of the White prisoners consider Spivey a race traitor. This fuels their hatred of him. Some Blacks dislike him because they believe he is out of place. Championing the attack on him was easy.

Before long Spivey is in a cell with one of his Crip brothers to be disciplined. Banging and slamming can be heard coming from the cell. It takes no more than five minutes. The two combatants emerge from the cell. Spivey has a swollen eye, but the man sent in to mete out discipline looks worse. Blood trickles from his lip.

The shot callers for DC and New York are not pleased. None of Spivey's blood has been shed. This prompts the Crip shot caller to call for a second round. The second time will likely be worse. It is.

Two Crip gang members go into the cell, Spivey in tow. One man stands in front of the cell door blocking any escape. The banging begins again. As I predicted, Round Two was less favorable to Spivey. The door is being slammed into. It's probably Spivey attempting to escape. The man holding the good looks in. Once he is satisfied by what he sees he moves away allowing Spivey to exit. Spivey comes out swinging his fists while his two attackers pursue him into the day room—one with a shiny piece of metal, the other with a padlock tied to a belt. Spivey retreats, his face a bloody mess, stab wounds to his neck and back. He stumbles to the guard's office in search of a reprieve. He yells for a nurse. The cop panics. Fumbling for his radio, he knocks it to the ground. The guard throws himself at the radio, grabs it with both hands, and hits the deuces. Once again staff members fill the unit. They order everyone to lock in. Surprisingly, everyone complies without protest. They know in the eyes of the decision makers this is a minor incident. This lock in won't last long.

Blood still dripping off him, Spivey addresses the unit. He's shouting.

"Ya'll a bunch of drama king ass bitches. Crying like suckas."

He walks out of the unit with his head down, a man wounded both physically and emotionally.

Figure 11 - Puddles of blood after a prisoner was stabbed and beaten.

What a brutal assault like this does to a man's mentality is interesting study. These attacks have turned many men paranoid. I have not faced a brutal assault but witnessing these assaults makes me wonder when someone is going to decide that I have done something wrong and deserve to be attacked. After all, this is Big Sandy. It has to happen at some point.

With the blood cleaned up, within an hour the cells are unlocked for us all to mingle. Tonight is *American Idol* night, something many prisoners enjoy. Even the tough guys bring their chairs and sit and watch the show. Like the rest, I park my chair in front of the television two times a week to tune in. The show is another small escape to a different place. Happiness, excitement, sadness, the program has all of these. Sometimes I slip off into a daydream. In those dreams I am at the show, singing along, clapping with the free people to the beat of the song. In reality though, I am still in my hard-plastic chair, my feet planted to the hard, cold concrete floor and the music is only zipping through my headphones.

I look around. I want to see my reality. Most of us are dead men walking. Life seems to have no meaning when you know the rest of it will be spent filled with violence, concrete, and blood. Once you give up nothing matters. When your life is gone, there is nothing anyone can do to hurt you. I say a silent prayer. I pray that I never tread those waters where I throw the towel in, where I quit on life. For now, my mind focuses on tasting freedom again. It's the only thing that keeps me walking forward each day. Like Nelson Mandela, I am on my own long walk to freedom.

There are only a few days of peace before the Aryan Brotherhood of Texas strikes at Dinky. A prisoner named Snow has been prospecting for the gang, under Dinky's tutelage. The only problem is Snow has a drinking problem. In his last drunken stupor he was disrespecting other White prisoners, saying stupid stuff. Because he was prospecting for the gang, instead of being beat up he was put on drinking restriction. Instead of following orders, he jumped right back inside the bottle and let that lead him down the road to verbally assaulting some Black prisoners. Those transgressions have stamped his ticket. The Blacks take their complaints to Dinky who promises them blood for the disrespect.

Snow has been a good prospect for the Aryan Brotherhood of Texas. Before anyone can join the gang, they must show their commitment to the group. They have to prove their loyalty. Proving oneself worthy is a matter of how much violence, or "work" someone "puts in" to further the gang's objectives. When Snow arrived, he was housed in Dinky's unit. That allowed Dinky to sink his claws into him. Prison is filled with manipulators. Manipulating Snow was easy. Dinky used him as a missile to wreak havoc on others. The circle has now come back to devour him. Two men Harley, and another prospect, Russ, are dispatched to avenge the Blacks being disrespected. Snow is found unconscious, beaten to a pulp. He is carted out of the unit on a stretcher, his head a massive, swollen mess. He has a one-way ticket off this lonely mountain of pain. He is leaving the same way he came in, with a big bang. Both Harley and Russ are led off to the SHU for their two weeks stay.

Figure 12 - Aryan Brotherhood tattoo.

Russ is now on a roll in his pursuit of obtaining a patch. He consistently racks up one violent act after another, in the name of the gang he has pledged an allegiance to. The Aryan Brotherhood of Texas.

When a prospect completes his probation period for the gang, if he is found deserving, a tattoo representing the gang is inked into his skin indicating he is an official, real-life, gang brother of this crew of misfits.

Violence has been on a fast-forward kind of trajectory this week. A guard has revealed to Dinky that a new prisoner from Texas is in for child pornography. There is a sick sense of excitement. Men salivate when these types of offenders take their chance on USP Big Sandy's battlefield. No mercy will be shown this unsuspecting victim. He has been convicted of committing the worst kind of crime. Victimizing an innocent child is reprehensible. I am perplexed as to why this man would try his luck. Some of these men have never been in trouble before so they do not know what checking in is, or how to do it. And I think some just want to die at someone else's hand; they lack the courage to take their own life.

Prison staff tend to dislike child molesters as much as the felons here on campus do. Staff members know what is in store for these men if they send them out on the compound. Staff still send them out with a pat on the back, and a silent, "Good luck." This is what happened with infamous Irish mob boss James "Whitey" Bulger in another federal prison. Staff sent him to the compound, casting him into a death pit where he did not last twenty-four hours.

The newspaper article is circulating. "Child Pornographer Sentenced in Dallas Court." One of the cops printed it off the internet. Dinky chooses one ABT gang member, a prospect, and an independent from Texas for this mission. The three assassins enter the housing unit the victim lives in. Like sonar, they lock their eyes on their intended target. Their icy glares freeze him. His instincts tell him they are here for him. The man moves fast, but he trips and stumbles to the ground. Somehow, he makes it back to his feet. Sneakers are squeaking against the freshly waxed floor. The chase begins. Almost as if on cue a guard exits the office and notices the three pursuers giving chase. He hits the deuces.

They close in on the sex offender; he is caught. They tackle him to the ground. His eyes indicate a reckless sense of fear for a split second, then he's stabbed. He looks like a zebra taken down by three ruthless lions bent on dismembering him. A shrieking squeal, like that of a stuck pig escapes from his lungs. Squirming under his attackers he swings wildly, fighting for his life. Punches and kicks to his head. Another knife appears. For some reason stab wounds are called hits, or shots in here. He's hit in the shoulder blade. Another shot punctures his cheek. There is a mad scramble. Somehow, he is back on his feet. His heart is pounding, you can see it. He takes off running again. Blood mixes with sweat and tears falling from his eyes. He runs around a table and up the stairs.

A swooshing sound fills the dayroom as staff rush in. The victim runs down the stairs. He's still being chased as he runs into the arms of a guard.

Staff wrestle the attackers to the ground. I see the depleted man through the officer's station window. He is on his knees crying into his hands, relieved that he still has his life. I think of the children he attacked. I mouth the words "Piece of shit," to myself as I lock my cell door before the cops do. When I turn around, Mr. Young is nodding his head.

"What do you think of that one there?" he asks.

"Ahh, I don't know. I guess he's a dirt ball," I answer.

"You know Chad, he deserved what he got. You know I don't like violence, but on a child molester? He got what his hand called for. I read the article. He was a real trash can that guy."

"Too bad they didn't kill him Mr. Young," I say harshly.

Mr. Young raises his eyebrows. "Nah son, he deserves to be brutalized from prison to prison. Death is too easy for that son of a bitch. You know they only give him twenty years for what he done?"

"Yah, I guess you're right. Death would be his way out. Twenty years of prison misery might serve him right."

"The case manager let me read some of his PSI. He was raping his own six-year-old daughter, recording it, and sending it to other people. Real sick puppy there Chad."

"He got less time than me," I say with anger in my voice.

"Oh, they don't give them Cho-mos what they deserve. If ya sell drugs they give ya forty years, if ya rape kids ya get half of that. Boy this government sure is stupid."

I nod in agreement. "Why the hell would they send him here?" I ask Mr. Young.

"Oh, they was hoping someone kill that son of a bitch," Mr. Young says, his face turning red with anger. Lately Mr. Young has been getting angrier at everything. His newfound anger brings increased cursing.

"Well, at least we won't be locked down too long," I say.

"We should be out soon. No one likes them damn Cho-mos. They was hoping someone killed him, trust me. That is why the cop printed that article. Hell, the case manager showed me his PSI on that computer back there. Told me ol' buddy was a piece of filth. She has kids herself."

"I don't understand how he thought it was alright to just sit around watching the television, or even coming out here on the yard."

"Some of 'em stupider than hell, Chad. They give it a try. Got their family making fake paperwork for 'em saying they're in for selling meth or something. What they don't think about is the staff here will tell their business. They do so much bullshit around here, they don't want no one telling on them. So they don't like the snitches or child molesters."

"You're right Mr. Young. When it comes to kids? Kids are innocent victims. Predators like that dude strip them of their innocence, their childhood. That scumbag raped his own kid because she was young, vulnerable, weak. Kids look to their parents to protect them. This cat was destroying his own kid. I think they should have killed him."

"Now that's where we differ Chad. Let 'em do about fifteen miserable years, then kill 'em."

We both laugh at Mr. Young's suggestion. We hear the hard metal sound of the doors being unlocked. I jumped down from the bunk knowing that the child molester was lucky to make it out of here today wounded rather than killed. When one of those men try their hand in a place like this, they will get their due, because everyone—staff and convicts—is working to make sure that goal is achieved.

TWENTY-SIX

WITHIN TWENTY MINUTES of being out of our cells, we are ordered to lock in. People are asking the guard the reason for the lockdown. They are told the Warden himself made the order because of the three separate issues of violence in one week. Locking us down is a way to punish the entire prison population. Stopping the violence is virtually impossible. The Warden's hope is that caging people up will calm them down. They'll appreciate being out of the cell. This thought process is just wrong. To prisoners here at Big Sandy, being locked in, losing privileges—this is all part of doing business. In a shot caller's mind, if a situation calls for violence, damn with the consequences. With no real incentive to behave, or to engage in rehabilitation, the violence will happen, and happen often.

It never takes long for depression to set in. When I am alone with my thoughts I often think of home, my family, my mother, my life before everything came crashing down. How long ago that was. These days now seem impossibly distant, the faintest recollections of a past life. A life that I no longer know. Thinking of that life, comparing it to this one, a feeling of sorrow wells up in my inner soul. What my life has become troubles me. I feel disgusted with myself for the choices I made. Like most men housed on this mountain, I fear that I might never leave this place. Each day is a mental struggle. The loneliness makes me tremble.

Blow up like the World Trade Center...

MY THEME SONG. By smoking crack Booper rescinded his position in our enterprise. I went from bagging up 62's to Big 8's to bigger things. Counting double digit thousand stacks made me happy. I was changing the trajectory of my life. The fast life was being kind to me—women, clothes, jewelry, cars. Being poor, struggling, those days were long gone. I had put them far behind me; what I never saw was that this sinister dungeon was my future. No one ever thinks about this part when the money is coming in, when life is good. At least I didn't. Big Sandy is part of being a drug dealer, it is an undesirable aspect, but it's all part of the package deal. Had I tasted even a little bit of this place I would have made a career change. I would have gone from drug dealer to whatever else is behind window number two. This is it. This is what my life is now.

MR. YOUNG IS making coffee prison style. Like all things this too is a process. A piece of fabric is cut from an old raggedy blanket Mr. Young keeps just for lock downs. It is about two feet long, eight inches wide. Once cut he rolls the fabric up into what he calls a bun. After cutting a small strip of aluminum off an oatmeal pack, he connects each end to a AAA battery creating a spark. He lights a small piece of toilet paper on fire. The toilet paper is his lighter—he uses it to light his bun on fire.

Mr. Young places the bun on the side of our toilet. This allows air to shoot up the middle of it. A soda can is filled with water and a long string is tied to the pull tab so he can hold the can over the open flames. Smelling the burning can and the smoke gives me an instant headache. It does nothing to the old man. My small cough makes Mr. Young look over his shoulder at me with a sly look.

"Well it ain't Starbucks son, but it's all I got," he says changing the sly look to a grin.

With my eyes burning, I respond, "Do you think toxins get in that water from the can being burned?"

"Chad, do you think I care much about toxins being in my water? This whole place is toxic to all of us," he responds succinctly before turning back to the flame.

Any chance of trying to talk Mr. Young into ceasing his coffee-making during lockdowns is out the door. He has to have his cup of joe, daily.

Three days of lockdown is our punishment for the violence. Not many men care. Seventy-two hours is nothing but a vacation for staff and cons. Victor is out of the SHU for his knife offense. Droopy took his place for five hundred dollars in cash. For the cash Droopy told the lieutenant that the shank belonged to him. When Vic was caught with the weapon, he had his transfer paperwork pending for a prison close to New York. A writeup would have halted the transfer. Getting close to home facilitates visits with family. The five hundred dollars is a small price to pay to visit with his loved ones. Everything in this prison is open to manipulation. Even getting caught red-handed with a knife. Staff only care that the documentation says that someone is held responsible for the killing instruments that are found. Droopy's payday only costs him twelve days in the SHU. Droopy's payday allows him to get high for free after his small vacation.

Things have been relatively calm for a few weeks since the last lockdown, but in a rare instance of solidarity many of the convicts are coming together over the quality of food as of late. The portions have become smaller. Food is comfort in prison. It is the one thing that everyone is concerned about, myself included. No one likes to be hungry. When a prisoner is hungry, they become angry, agitated. With agitation comes problems. Just weeks ago there was a self-serve hot bar always stocked with rice, beans, and soup. Some men lived off rice and beans; that has vanished. The cold bar that once held salad, vegetables, and other small things to eat has also disappeared. According to the food administrator, the food budget was over a hundred thousand dollars in the red. Slashing the extras was his way of fixing the problem.

Most men in here have little to no money. With the food cuts it means they will be going to bed hungry. What that means for the prison is anyone's guess. I suspect more empty stomachs will lead to an increase in robberies which will in turn increase the violence. I go to sleep thinking of the repercussions that will come as a result of the declining food situation. Keeping my eye on my belongings is a top priority.

Today I wake up to what will be one of the worst days I will ever see in prison. I do not realize it until months later, but it is the start to my end on this mountain. Although they do not reside in this unit they are here; Adam with Dennis, and Ronnie behind them. Immediately I'm contemplating whether I've violated any prison rules. I search my mind wondering if I told anyone how much I dislike Steve. I come up empty, but I still have a nervous feeling in my stomach. It's abnormal for all three of them to be in this unit. My eyes search for Frank. In my haste I do not notice him just feet away. Like myself he is watching them. Their eyes lock on us. They approach, my mouth is parched, senses heightened as nervousness overcomes me. When they get closer Adam sticks his hand out. "What's up homeboy? Why you look so paranoid?" he asks.

Given everything I have observed since coming here I become leery if anything is out of tune even a slight bit, suspicious of people's real motives. I play things cool and shake Adam's hand.

"What the hell are you talking about? Paranoid? I ain't paranoid." I laugh it off to mask the truth he saw on my mug. "What's up though? You three aren't here for no reason."

"Yah, you're right. We need you and Frank to move to our unit bro."

"Why?" I ask, curious.

"Some dudes got locked up in our unit. We don't want to lose any White cells with all these Mexicans coming here. We got empty cells we have to fill."

Noticing my reluctance Ronnie interjects, "Look, Adam is your homeboy. You can go in a cell with him. Frank can go in a cell with me. As soon as we can work it out, you and Frank can get a cell together."

Ronnie's explanation does not add up, prompting me to respond, "I thought you said there were open cells now?"

"There were, but we put some dudes in them for now to hold them down. But if you guys don't move they're going to make the White dudes with no cell mates move in together, and then we're going to lose White cells," Ronnie retorts. He sounds demanding, sarcasm floating off this tongue. He is angry that I would even challenge him; as if we are little kids, obliged to do what they say without objection. My mind is made up. I don't like Ronnie either. In reality, me and Frank are being used so that Adam and Ronnie can keep their cells. They want us to save them from having to move in with each other. I don't want to move. To me, living with the top dogs in the car is a recipe for disaster. The more people together from the car, the more potential for issues. Frank and I are as comfortable as you can be while in prison in our unit. Mr. Young is in my peripheral vision shaking his head, as if he's willing me to say no. Really though, refusing really isn't an option. If we refuse it will cause animosity. Against my better judgment, I lamely agree to move to their housing unit. Saying no would have caused our ranking in the hierarchy of the car to tumble precipitously. The next time that car needed work put in, Frank and I would have been called on to be the missiles. My position in the car is maintained simply because I am from New York; the Irish descent helps as well. Those two things can only carry me so far. How far is up for debate.

Frank's initial dislike for Steve is slowly fading. Steve's stories have begun to mesmerize him. He's falling into the snake's grasp. He is beginning to dance to Steve's every tune, a hypnotized cobra before an Indonesian man playing his instrument.

The sad, empty feeling has come again. Moving always messes up my nerves. Not knowing what lies ahead does it to the best of men. Leaving Mr. Young bothers me as well. My head down, I go to my cell to pack my belongings. Making the best out of a bad situation is the only option I really have.

I look up to see Mr. Young staring intently at me.

"What did they want?"

"They want us to move downstairs so they don't lose White cells, or some shit."

"I ain't moving downstairs with them son of a—"

I put up my hand to stop Mr. Young. "Not you. Me and Frank."

"Did I not tell you not to get involved with those clowns from the start? But you chose not to listen to the old man, right?"

"Come on with this shit! Now is not the time," I answer angrily.

"Why don't ya just tell 'em you was comfortable here? That you wasn't moving boy?"

"It don't work that way Mr. Young. You know it don't."

"Bullshit. You got forty years. Stand up to them son of a bitches." Mr. Young points his finger at me. His voice rises.

"Then what? They punch my head off?"

"If you would have listened to me from jump street, you wouldn't be in this position now. Now would ya?"

I get angry in an instant. I stand up. I point my finger back at Mr. Young. "You're an old man. Things work differently for younger guys in here. I am an asset to them dudes. I'm from New York. No way were they going to let me stay here and be on my own. If I refused the car, they might not have stabbed me, but they would have beat the shit out of me. Because you're old with no money, no one fucks with you. My problems are bigger than yours."

He is shaking as he responds. He is like a father scolding an unruly child. "Get your shit and get the hell out of here! Remember this young man. I told you so! Don't forget that I told you so!"

Mr. Young leaves our cell, with a slam of the door. Well *his* cell now.

Fucking prison. This is prison. This is where these dirty mother fuckers sent me for forty years. In my heart I know I just don't have forty years in me. I know I don't—I just cannot do forty years in here.

Reluctantly, I move my things into Adam's cell. It looks like a cyclone has been through here. The comfortable feeling of living in a clean cell with the old man… I'm probably not going to have that again. Once again Big Sandy teaches me small things matter. This new cell looks like a junk yard. Within minutes I miss the shiny waxed floors that Mr. Young was so meticulous about, the sparkling clean toilet and sink, and the small knickknacks. My new home is adorned with scuff marks on the wall because Adam's cell is a makeshift wrestling ring for the guys in the car. Prison-issued black boots are what cause the black scars on the off-white paint. Books are in disarray, clothing strewn throughout the cell, dried toothpaste on the mirror, hair in the sink from Adams excessive brushing of his long, black hair. The living quarters looks more like a teenager's room in his parent's basement than a maximum-security federal prison cell.

With an uneasy feeling in my new house, I commit to myself to keep my bed made, and my property neatly tucked away in my assigned locker until I can escape this situation. Everything in prison has a price, even cells. A guy who lives alone, finding himself in debt, or desperate to get high will sell his cell for a price. If he finds another guy living alone that he can move in with, he will sell his cell and split the profit with the other guy. Cells go from two hundred to five hundred dollars. Real estate shopping is now a priority; in fact, looking around this cell once again, it's my first priority. But finding a cell to buy is not an easy task; you have to catch the right person, at the right time.

Both Frank and I make our rounds in the unit. We greet all the homeboys with fake smiles, at least I do. Frank is falling for Steve's manipulation little by little. Me, I'm going through the motions. I feel dead without being dead. Given my dislike for Steve, moving into this unit is like flirting with death. At least twenty guys in the car live in this unit. Most occupy cells upstairs in the back corner of the unit. If Steve called on them to attack, they would rip me apart like a pack of wolves. I'm going to have to be very careful with what I say, very careful with what I do. To say I feel trapped makes a mockery of understatement. I am in prison inside a prison. There are some other White prisoners living in the unit with us. To my surprise, they are gang members. Imagine that, living under the same roof in close proximity to their number one hater.

I know two of these men. Joe is a SAC gang member. SAC stands for Soldier of Aryan Culture. His cell mate is a young man named T.J. who was once a Hammerskin. Today he is prospecting to be a part of the Aryan Brotherhood, or Brand. T.J. does not know it now, but he is marching toward a somnolent fate, already sealed. He came to prison with what convicts would call a short sentence. He will never be a free man again. He will never leave prison. He will move up the ladder for his gang by killing another convict, and with this deliberate act seal his own destiny.

These gang members coexist with us inside this concrete jungle we inhabit for as long as Steve remains sensible. If he drops the hammer, or calls the shot, we would decimate our rivals. If the gang members ever have the hand that Steve has now, there would be no hesitation on their part; they would attack us. I'm perplexed. Why doesn't Steve make his move? Perplexed but relieved as well. I really want to make it out of this place alive it that is possible. The air crackles with the tension between us and them. Their only problem is there are many more of us than them, they know they would be on the losing end if they made the wrong move. Nobody has to say this out loud, but I know that if the numbers change, things will get ugly quickly. They hate Steve as much as he hates them.

Dennis lives in the back cell, three cells from our cell. Like Red, Dennis runs his own tattoo shop making good prison money. Similarly, he also has a penchant for heroin which sucks up his profits leaving his locker bare—no food, no necessities. Heroin in his veins like a fish in the sea. It chases away his misery, the loneliness that hits all men on this side of the razor wire like a cannon direct and broadside. The picture is slowly being formed. I see Steve, Adam, Dennis, and Ronnie for what they are—men who have formed a car that benefits them.

This is the wheel of prison turning, devouring, depleting the men in the car for whatever resources they have to offer. Steve is like an amusement ride conductor at the helm, cranking the lever of evil. After two weeks in this unit I can see things ever more clearly.

TO MY DISSATISFACTION, the prison real estate market has not been kind to me.

New White gang members have arrived on the bus. Our unit has been gifted two, tattooed Aryan Brotherhood of Texas gang members. Steve, always the weird, paranoid man is not happy about the new arrivals, not happy they live amongst us. His propaganda machine is running full throttle. He fills the soldiers' heads with fear, warning all of us, daily, to keep our eyes and ears open. Steve instructs us to keep our knives on us at all times. Living in this unit has spiked my stress levels on account of the fear of what might happen to me or what I might have to do to sustain my own life.

Judges, prosecutors, Congress, no one knows what is really going on here. If they did, maybe someone would shut this place down. Start over. Culture change. All manner of problems, and death, and violence find people in here; people who aren't looking for any of it. One of the three are always knocking at my door no matter how much I want to avoid them—I am afraid to answer the door but the way time works, I know it is inevitable. This is a for sure thing. That peaceful cell with Mr. Young is long gone, and dearly missed.

Am I dreaming? Boom! Boom! Boom!

Banging—echoing in my mind. It reverberates off the metal bed frame. There it is again. Boom! Boom! Boom!

My sleep is interrupted. The loud banging is at my door. Wiping my eyes, I focus on my watch. It is 4:30 p.m. Both of us fell asleep during the 4:00 p.m. count. I look to the cell door's window to see a face staring into our darkened room.

"Adam, I need you to turn the light on for me," comes the voice at the door.

"What? What's the problem now?" Adam hollers back while still laying in his bunk.

"I need the light on. I need to talk to you."

"Adam, it's the lieutenant," I say after making out his white shirt, and the metal bars on his collar.

"Are you fucking kidding me?" Adam yells at the door. Groggy, he stands up, makes his way to the light, and flicks on the switch.

"What?" he shouts spreading his arms out. "What the fuck do you want?"

Trying to be polite, the lieutenant says, "We need you and your cell mate to cuff up for us."

"What the fuck for jerk off?" Adam yells back. Adam explodes like the Fourth of July. Looking at me he says, "There's a bunch of asshole cops out here."

"Adam, the warden wants us to lock you, Steve, Dennis, and Ronnie up for a few days. This ain't my call, I'm just doing my job."

Steve yells out through the crack in his door. "Adam, fuck them! We're going hard! Get the team! Go get your goon squad."

Steve has given the sacred order to fight back against the staff, setting Adam off like a madman out of control. Adam unleashes a barrage of threats, promises, and curses at the cops standing on the other side of the door. Looking at me he raises his eyebrows, "Chad you ready to go hard?"

"Man, it's whatever," I respond. Not because it's how I really feel, but it's the only answer. The last thing I want to do is engage in a physical altercation with the guards. It is the lesser of the two evils though. The cops won't stab me. The car will. Again, I'm damned if I do, and damned if I don't.

"Chad if they come in here, I'm stabbing them."

This is not what I signed up for. My fake confidence wavers. Now I'm hoping that somehow, someone can talk these guys down before things get any further out of control. Someone has to fold their hand. If Steve refuses, me and Adam are getting gassed with a super soaker filled with mace. The Captain is at Steve's door explaining that this is over different cars taking ownership of cells. He says the warden is only locking them up for a few days along with some other shot callers from various groups. The warden wants to talk to the prison bosses of the cars. Other prisoners are riled up now, kicking their cell doors, egging on the disturbance. No one can get a word in causing staff to fold; in frustration they leave the unit. Once they're gone the noise diminishes.

Steve calls to Adam. "Listen, I think we should go ahead, go over there so we don't lose the cells. If they Team us, they won't let us out of the hole."

"The Captain said a couple of days before the warden talks to us, so whatever you want to do. You make the call. Me and Chad are ready for whatever," Adam yells back.

"Alright. This is what we will do. Leave our cellies here to hold the cells down. If that is the agreement we leave peacefully. If not, we go full throttle."

To my relief it looks like this thing is going to end peacefully. I hope. Adam looks at me with a serious face and instructs me to get all the guys together as soon as the doors are unlocked and let them know to be on point. He also tells me that we have to stay strapped with weapons. Adam speculates that the gang members might make a move on us now that the top guys will be in the SHU. The homemade blind goes up on our window so no one can see into our cave. Adam shows me a fake shelf he has in his locker. I knew it was there just never took a look for myself.

He pries open the shelf, exposing a six-inch gap that reveals his secret stash. Inside seven bone crushers are tucked away from prying eyes.

"Listen Chad, don't show no one this spot, or tell anyone about it. Make sure all the brothers have a weapon. Do not sleep on these gang dudes. If they get out of line, kill 'em, cause they will kill you bro."

"Alright man, I got you. I will make sure everyone is armed," I say nodding in agreement. Nervousness makes my stomach quiver. Confused and scared, I realize that prison is about to get real. Moving to this unit placed me in a position where I'm already reaping the consequences I feared, consequences I never wanted to be manifested. These instruments of destruction have been in this cell since my arrival. I am amazed at the hiding spot. It is fashioned from a shelf ripped out of another locker that fits perfectly over the top of Adam's bottom shelf.

"Two other guys in the unit know about the hiding spot Chad. Don't trip. Both are trustworthy." I take the trustworthy comment with a grain of salt. From my own experiences no one is trustworthy in prison. Being in this cell with this cache of weapons bothers me. The last thing I want to do is be caught with this steel. I try to avoid problems. My appeal is still pending. Instead I am tossed into a fire. I pray I don't get burned.

The blind comes off the window when the cops return with Ms. L., the associate warden. She is attractive for an older woman. She knows how to deal with violent, angry men. Ms. L. has a reputation for being respectful, as well as honest. She promises Steve that if he comes out peacefully no one will be in the SHU longer than a week. After some jockeying and compromising in a lame effort to save face, Steve sticks his skinny arms through the slot and cuffs up. He is the first to be led out. After the king exits, his political cabinet follows. Adam, Dennis, and Ronnie are all taken to the SHU. The car is left with no leadership.

Once the doors are unlocked, we are summoned into Steve's room by his cellmate Jimmy. Steve has left him a game plan for the car. We are all told to stay in groups of three, everyone armed with a weapon. Also, no one can get drunk or high while our leaders are away. The men seem jittery, creating their own tension. I try to stay calm. Staying calm allows me to think clearly, it allows me to be aware of those around me. The younger guys in the car want to provoke an issue with the White gang members. They believe conquering them would make Steve proud.

I voice my opinion. "Thinking rationally without provoking a physical altercation is in all of our best interest," I tell the misfits. "Our main goal is to make sure all four men make it out of the hole. If we provoke an issue this will not happen, and it would piss Steve off." The misguided agree. Everyone is now armed with a steel pipe, or knife. We still have the numbers in our favor. There are some heavy hitters among our ranks. It would be a mistake for the gang members to move on us. The lions reign supreme, they are hyenas. They despise this reality, but they do not allow ignorance to overcome their intelligence.

While gang members in federal prison are used to asserting their power over every other White prisoner in these confines, the Independent movement has stifled their control. I had a false misconception about White gang members before entering these doors. I thought they were about their race, about lifting up their own, living righteously. I was wrong. They pilfer, extort, and rob their own for the most part, simply to get high.

Steve is doing the same thing, just not as extreme. He says he stands against the gang members. Yet he commits oppression through manipulation. Fearmongering is his preferred tool. That's what he uses to achieve his goals.

My first order of personal business is to clean the cell. Adam's absence allows me to remove the scuff marks. Walls, floors, and the mirror are cleaned. The toilet sparkles like Mr. Young's. When the cell locks, I can lay back comfortable. Sucking in the alone time relieves some pressure. I am, in my solitude, finding some moments of contaminated peace. I slide a bone crusher under my pillow. My first night along in Big Sandy makes me giddy in an absurd way.

CHAPTER

TWENTY-SEVEN

SIX DAYS LATER, Steve, Adam, and Dennis are back without
Ronnie "tough guy" Wilson. When the warden went to talk to
Ronnie, he was belligerent. He told the warden to go screw his
mother. To celebrate their return, Adam is cooking us a meal. Rice,
summer sausage, pepperoni, refried beans, with cold sodas. Because of
his generosity, we skip the mess hall and gather in Steve's cell for a
small meeting among the top convicts in the car.

A meeting of some sort is scheduled with the Warden, Steve, Adam,
and the same Captain who told me to get a knife. The Federal Bureau
of Prisons has been shipping Sureños to Big Sandy by the bus load.
There have been issues with cells, leaving the Hispanic gang members
with no cells to call their own. The aim of this meeting is to have the
cars relinquish a cell or two in each unit. If the shot callers refuse, the
warden will simply lock the bosses up, and ship them to new prisons.

Steve promises that if the warden gets out of line, he is going to
commit some sort of violence. It goes in one ear, out the other. False
bravado to make the soldiers think Steve is their prison God. When
things got real a few days ago he cuffed up and took the easy way out.
At the meeting he will take the same course of action, I am sure.

Adam's decisions are more rash, void of any thoughtful calculations or consideration of consequences. Anything is possible with Adam. Living in a cell with Adam is dangerous for me, but it's Big Sandy—everything is dangerous here.

The morning comes, and goes, with no trouble. As I anticipated, Steve is nothing more than talk. I am getting the sense that the gang members think Steve is phony as well. Watching my own back is my priority. I can no longer count on Frank. He is dancing the fiddler's dance to Steve's every tune.

Leo, a new Boston guy has arrived with troubles from his past. Leo is half Black, half White with the word "Skinhead" tattooed on his head. He is running with our car which, like most things here, confuses me. Upon his arrival he spotted a Black Boston guy that he once had beef with back in the county jail. Leo wants to book the guy—stab him. Because of his old beef we are summoned to the yard to hold Leo down.

Steve has embraced Leo as a Boston brother given his defection from gang life. Given how bright the sun shines, I lift my sunglasses to make sure what I am seeing is real. Leo, knife in hand, is chasing the Black prisoner through the yard. If I can so easily see this, I wonder how the cops cannot. Maybe they don't want to see it. Like a lot of things that get ignored here.

The Black kid is running like a wild jack rabbit. He zigzags, trying to get away from Leo. The kid's offense happened four years ago. He told Leo to go fuck himself, and his White mother. Both men were in the SHU, separated by steel doors. Leo feels this infraction deserves a good stabbing. No thought goes into what the repercussions will be for the Whites if he stabs a Black convict.

Standing in the middle of the yard, unarmed, I have no clue what will happen if Leo catches his target. But I am ready to protect myself if I have to. Except for a few of us, Leo, and the Jack Rabbit, no one seems to know what is going on. Why the Jack Rabbit has not looked to his people for refuge bewilders me. Steve intervenes. He calls Leo over to our circle. It is obvious he cannot catch the young Jack Rabbit.

Steve explains that this whole thing is foolish. Steve has picked up some intelligence somewhere. This surprises me.

He proposes a solution, whereby, the two of them approach the Black Boston shot caller to set up a one on one duel. Leo insists on a knife fight. I get the feeling that Leo does not want to settle his dispute with old-fashioned fisticuffs. Rumor is he got knocked out at USP Lee by a country boy named Koon which resulted in his transfer here. His protests trigger Adam's anger. In another thoughtless decision, Adam tells me and Frank that if Leo does not listen, he is going to kill him. Armed with his bone crusher I know Adam is not faking. He will do exactly what he has promised without so much as blinking an eye.

Leo finally realizes that knuckling up is his only real option if the Blacks will agree. The jack rabbit's name is Anthony. He's not looking for a fight, but his shot caller insists he has to square off. The two combatants meet in the middle of the yard where wild punches between the two men are exchanged. More misses than connections before the P.A. system squawks to life. The instructions I have come accustomed to blare from the speakers. Instinctively, I go to the ground on one knee. The first of two shotgun blasts echoes off the concrete. Warning shots. Within minutes of the first punch, both cons are tackled to the ground, cuffed, and led off to the SHU.

No one leaves this fight victorious on the judges' cards. Neither of the combatants were good with their hands. The house of hard knocks has a lot of men who do not know how to fight with their bare knuckles. With little to no skills, the same men have no reservations about stabbing others. No one wants to be on the losing end of a prison fight—sticking someone with steel is the equalizer. Weapons give cons confidence here at Big Sandy. Not much of a fighter, Leo wanted this to be a knife fight. After watching the carnival boxing contest, I know why that was his first choice.

Living conditions with Adam have improved dramatically. I have learnt the skill of dealing with him. There is a mutual respect being formed between him and I. Adam is not half as bad as I thought although I know now that he is slightly crazy. Like most of us Adam came in young with a severe sentence. He has a fourteen-year sentence in the federal system, with another twenty-year term in New York when his federal sentence is complete. Sadly, some people break under the pressure of sentences as draconian as these. Living with Adam it is clear—sadly, again—that he has given up on life outside of prison. Prison is his life; it is all that matters.

Not long after the Leo incident we end up with a new guy from Texas who wants to be in our car. Preston came from another prison, and like us he despises the White gang members. In only a few weeks Adam and Preston form a close friendship. Both prisoners like getting drunk. They have also been indulging in heroin, the forbidden fruit. Preston has no bunk mate so when the two get a batch of wine done, Adam sleeps over at Preston's house. They drink, argue, and wrestle all night long as if they are teenagers all over again. Sleepovers in prison. Sometimes I have no idea where I am.

Hanging out with Preston has precipitated Adam's downward spiral. Drinking coupled with heroin use has become part of his daily calendar. It consumes his lonely existence. It's his way of escaping the demons that haunt us, always reminding us that this is our home. We are not here just for a year or two. We are here for the best parts of our life— maybe forever. As his life spirals out of control my focus remains on my own legal appeal. Adam lost all his appeals long ago. As he has told me many times, once I lose all my legal remedies I will accept my fate. He does not know what I know. Losing is not an option for me. I will never stop fighting for my freedom.

The car is growing like a well-fed baby. What once began as a Boston-New York car, has slowly morphed into an all-around White Independent car as Steve is taking in more members from all over the United States. Strength comes in numbers, Steve likes strength. One of his newest members is Chuck from North Carolina. With Adam's help, Steve is laying a scam down on Chuck. Steve instructs Chuck to have his family send four hundred dollars to another prisoner's family—

ostensibly to purchase heroin. The way Chuck thinks it works is Chuck will get twenty individual papers of heroin that he can sell at five prison books of stamps a piece.

In reality, Steve is getting one gram of heroin for Chuck's money. With one gram he makes forty-five papers, gives Chuck his twenty, and pockets the rest. Their main goal is to hook their fish, get him to develop a habit of his own so they can slowly milk him for everything he has. It's easy to despise this false brotherhood the more it becomes evident that the top dogs are doing exactly what they say the gang members are doing. I am being led by men who scam their own people. Everyone in the car is disposable but Steve—even Adam. No matter your position, when Steve decides to throw you into the ocean with the sharks he will.

No matter what United States Penitentiary you are in, every car operates this way. Only the strong survive. Sometimes even the strong get chewed up, swallowed, and regurgitated. Trying to make it out of prison is a twenty-four-hour, seven-days-a-week job. Not only must you be physically strong, you need mental strength beyond comprehension. You have to be intelligent enough to decipher everything that is going on in the environment. If you don't possess these skills, at some point you become shark bait. Simple.

The White gang members have been building courage—courage fueled by anger. The Aryan Resistance Militia (ARM) gang leaders have called for a meeting with Steve and Adam. We have over a hundred men from our car stationed on the yard, at the ready if anything goes wrong. The men are doing what we call politicking. To me it is more like bickering. Deep inside I am hoping that something breaks out between us and the ARM guys. If it does, that's my ticket out of here, my chance for a new start somewhere else. It would be a blessing to get away from Steve. I have two bocce balls at my feet that I won't hesitate to throw. Perhaps I can hit Steve and claim it was an accident. The thought makes me the only man smiling on the yard.

A.J., the leader of ARM. has voiced his displeasure with the fact that

Steve is taking all the White independents into his fold as soon as they arrive. In a respectful way he claims we are taking in lames and giving them protection. Lames are guys who are nobodies, guys who under normal circumstances would be scared of their own shadow. Lacking backup, the lames are perfect prey for gangs to steal from, to oppress. They want the lames swimming alone in these rough waters with the piranhas.

Steve stands strong, courage unwavering with our support behind him. Forcefully, he makes it clear that this is our yard, that we are going to do what we want, when we want. Always ready for violence, Adam makes it known that the ball is in their court. All they have to do is make a move. I am in earshot. I hear the exchanges.

My guess is ARM came to this meeting ready to spark a clash. Once again, our members have stolen the day. Outmaneuvered and overwhelmed, they have tucked their tails, swallowed their pride, forced to abandon whatever plan they may have had. For a fleeting moment I think about chucking one of the bocce balls at a gang leader to set off a melee. I am disappointed nothing physical transpired. This was my one-way ticket out of humanity's sick joke—USP Big Sandy. I am here with my pent-up anger and my clenched fist. The longer he waits to pull the trigger, the more danger Steve puts us all in. If the numbers turn, unlike us, the gang members will not hesitate to inflict punishment. They may even get tired of being backed into a corner with only one way out. They might not wait to get their numbers up. They might decide instead that the only way to win is to attack two or three of us when we are separated from the group.

As much as I hate Steve, my hatred for White gangs is stronger. It is a learned behavior that has been embedded in me. Prison has finally taken its toll on me. I too am broken, not all the way, but close. The cold-heartedness of this life is biting at my soul. Slowly I calcify. Like others, I want to lash out, to hurt the convicts who really want to hurt me. Will their blood bring me peace? These hostile thoughts are born, bred in prison. For some men they grow slowly, faster for others.

Over time prison will destroy a person morally, mentally, and emotionally. I am experiencing this very thing. I am screaming out from the inside. It's hard for me to fathom how people with grotesque sentences, no family, and nothing to look forward to continue to live day by day in this prison life. Some commit suicide to escape the torment, others push forward, somehow, someway. Maybe Adam is right. If I lose my appeals, I might accept prison as my fate. But, accepting prison will be the day that I transform into an uncompromising beast. Losing your appeals is the end of the road. Once that is lost there is nothing left to lose. At that point I will have lost everything making prison my forever home. Silently, I pray I never cross that road.

The night sky is moving in as we walk back into the building. I look up at the clouds, the same ones from a few months ago, before I step into the doorway. He is darker this time, no longer laughing at me. He chuckles instead. I scowl back and throw two middle fingers toward the clouds, prompting Adam to laugh.

"What the hell you doing Chad?" Adam asks

"Man, just saying good night to the man," I reply.

Adam has no idea about the guy in the clouds. Only I can see him.

TWENTY-EIGHT

THE NIGHT IS STILL YOUNG when we make it back to our dorm. Wine is flowing freely. People in the car indulge, kind of celebrating. Steve letting the gang members know who's boss. When the devil's drink is in abundance, he seems to show up to pour the wine himself and mixes violence in.

Dave, a lame from Rhode Island, has had too much to drink. He is standing on the top tier of our housing unit, blatantly calling people niggers. His drunkenness has clouded his rational thinking. Dave is oblivious to the fact that he has just signed a contract authorizing a brutal assault on his person. Throwing blatant racial epithets at unsuspecting victims jeopardizes everyone's safety. The problem must be dealt with immediately.

Black prisoners are looking up at Dave, fangs dripping saliva, thirsty for fresh meat. The Blacks respect Adam. Even without words being said they know punishment is coming. Steve quickly ushers Dave into his cell, soothing him with kind words to calm him down in his drunken stupor. He does not recognize Steve's boiling anger, or what his impending future holds.

After small talk between Steve, and Adam, they call Frank, me, and another guy named Coffee into Dennis' cell.

"Listen, I need you three. You guys are on deck it's time now."

Frank responds, "What do you want us to do?"

"You can stab him, or lock him, it's up to you guys. But you got to fuck him up. If not, we are going to have a race riot in here."

I speak immediately to head off any dumb assertions that we should stab Dave. "I'm not stabbing him Adam! I'll just go in there and knock his ass out," I say.

Coffee, like me, doesn't want to be involved in stabbing anyone. He nods his head.

"He has to get smashed. These Blacks want to see blood," Adam responds.

"Not a problem bro! We got it," Coffee exclaims in an excited voice.

"Steve wants an example set, so when the C.O. walks out for the recreation move, go in there and get that son of a bitch."

"Alright," I respond.

"Frank and Jimmy are going to hold the door. Keep him in his room until then. Chad, you and Coffee are going in. Frank, you're the backup, kid."

The plan is laid out. My nerves are jumping, I am anxious to unleash the fury bottled up inside me. Pacing back and forth I wait for the recreation call. My black, leather work-out gloves slide over my hands. Dave is a dope fiend. Like so many others he intravenously injects the poison. I want to avoid his blood getting on my hands.

"Recreation Move! Let's go!" the guard yells as he exits the unit.

My arms are instantly heavy. My heart races and my palms begin to sweat under the leather. Coffee follows behind me as we enter Dave's chamber.

"Dave my friend! What's up with your language? You know the nigger word!" I yell.

"Man, fuck them nig..." Before he can finish the word, I hit him dead center in his mouth. Blood gushes from his busted lips and he stumbles backwards into the lockers with a loud, "Ahh." I unleash a flurry of punches until he falls to the floor. Coffee is kicking Dave in the face. I hold Dave on the ground with one hand while punching him in the back, and the ribs with the other. Screams for help cannot save him.

"Stop! I'm sorry! That's it, that's enough," he cries out.

"No. This is what you wanted when you were calling people niggers, punk," I howl out as one punch after another connects.

"Don't kill me, bro. I got kids man."

"Fuck you, and your kids," Coffee barks back.

Some time later I come out of my anger trance. Chest heaving, breath strained, I give Coffee the look: Dave has had enough. Blood is on my shirt, gloves, and on the locker. With one hand on the locker Dave lifts himself from the cold floor. His face is a bloody mess.

"Get the fuck out of here you piece of shit. You could have got us all killed" I say before spitting in his face.

Frank and Jimmy step aside as Dave escapes, running full force towards the guard's office. Handing my gloves to Jimmy my eyes connect with Steve's from across the room. He gives me a wink and a nod, as if he is praising me for a job well done. Little does he know that given the opportunity he would be punished in the same way, perhaps worse. The assault on Dave was done simply to avoid the White prisoners from being massacred by the Blacks. The bone I would like to pick with Steve is personal. Motivated by what he is doing to all of us. Hiding my true feelings, I nod back.

Once at the bottom of the stairs, Dave stops to look up at us. He screams out in anger, "Look at what you did to me you White bitches! Look at me!"

He shouts this with defeat, and shame in his voice. He looks like Roberto Duran in the "No Mas" fight with Sugar Ray Leonard. One eye swollen shut, lips busted, his face decorated with speed knots, and his broken nose dripping like a faucet. He starts to yell out again. Frank appears out of nowhere and delivers a football kick to Dave's ass. As the guard exits his office Dave begins to run. Frank latches on to his shirt striking him in the back.

By now the deuces are hit. In comes the goon squad to pin Frank to the wall. Once pinned down, the cops cuff him and haul him off to SHU. He had to take one for the team. Sometimes being the backup guy costs more. When Dave started yelling, Adam gave Frank the order to attack. That costs him a few days in the SHU. In this hell hole that's a small price to pay for the good of the car.

We are locked in our cells for body searches. The cops go from cell to cell requiring everyone to take their shirts off. They're searching for marks, stab wounds, or scratches. Any wounds on a person gives guards the authority to put people in the SHU for an investigation. We have already flushed my blood-stained shirt down the toilet.

I look out the window to see Coffee being led away in cuffs. He failed the body inspection test. Dave scratched Coffee's arm in the scuffle.

"Adam, am I straight? Do I got any marks?" I ask hoping the answer is no.

"Take your shirt off, you scary mother fucker."

"I ain't scared. Just not trying to go to the SHU."

"You're good. Your hand is a little bit swollen. Just flip your hands over quick, I'll start talking to the cops to get their attention on me. Off your hands."

Luck has found me. We are checked. I slide through the inspection. Adam engages the inspectors in conversation. About 6'4", 275 pounds, Adam's presence alone grabs people's attention. I will not be joining Frank and Coffee this evening. In a sick way it felt good to finally release my pent-up anger. Putting work in for a car I dislike so much fuels my disgust. Reasoning with myself, I conclude it was okay to do this to avoid any racial tension. My safe existence means I must go through the motions. The reality is we prisoners are dropped into a ready-made, built-in dynamic that leads to hatred for the people around us. Rather than coming together for good we alienate each other, all while pretending we have a brotherhood in place.

After the round up they unlock our doors are again. Pats on the back for a job well done come in droves. Praise from guys in the car, as well as from some of the Black convicts. In a normal society it would be abnormal to be applauded for such brutality. In prison these actions are worthy of praise. Like a chameleon, I am blending in with the rest of the fakers.

I am transforming into one of them—a cold-hearted prisoner. My subconscious mind is telling me not succumb to my environment. But I am knocking on the door, while fighting the beast—the prison beast that destroys young men like me. But really, my eyes are set on Steve.

TWENTY-NINE

"BLOWN UP LIKE you thought I would, call the crib, same number, same hood, it's all good."

I sing my old school theme song while I add baking soda to the Pyrex. Like a chemist I turn powder into crack, and like a magician, crack into cash. Who would have ever thought I would be using a microwave to concoct my new nefarious product?

"Why you always singing that same shit?" my best friend, E, asks.

"'Cause I like it, dog."

"That shit's old son."

"Man, do you think I care?" I say pulling the Pyrex from the microwave. I drop ice cubes in the boiling water. The cocaine hardens into crack. I don't like this next part. Bagging up the product for street sales. With four crack houses pumping high volume I know me and E will be at the table for hours.

"Look, you put the bags together E, I'll bag up the eight balls."

"Must be nice to be the boss," he says sarcastically.

Like scores of drug addicts I have become addicted to the life, the power that comes with being, as E puts it, the boss. We were doomed before we were born. Relegated to parents who are lifelong Ghost Town residents, never realizing that my surroundings would dictate my future. Violence, poverty, abuse, and addiction—all too much to overcome.

Each bag I fill with crack might as well be a day in prison. I have filled many bags never thinking about Big Sandy. Hell, I never heard of the place. How could I think about it?

Fate knows Big Sandy, Chad does not. One day I will.

"Blown up like you thought I would. .. "

"You singing the same line dog."

"Yah cause we're blown up E. Sit back. Relax. We counting double digit thousand stacks."

E laughs at me and we finish packaging our neighborhood's desires.

CHAPTER

THIRTY

THE FEDERAL BUREAU OF PRISONS has banned all pornographic material. With pornography expelled a new phenomenon has erupted behind these walls. Men have been masturbating while looking at fully clothed female staff. At times they will pull their penis out of their pants, and stroke in front of women with no shame. Prisoners call this "gunning."

Guys will stand in a classroom window, or sit at a desk pleasuring themselves while a female teacher teaches GED. Some resort to wilder, but more discreet, antics. They tie a piece of dental floss to their toe, and the other end to their penis. All they have to do is bounce the tied foot up and down as if tapping to any ol' tune, all while lusting in their mind.

No woman is off limits to the gunner—looks, age, nothing matters. They have no concern that this person is someone's mother, sister, or daughter. Not even grandmothers are off limits to these sexually deviant men. While most women do not invite these shameful sins, some do. It is rumored that one case manager, Ms. C., will watch men masturbating in the SHU through the small glass windows on the cell doors. The mill says sometimes she licks her lips, sometimes she smiles, sometimes she comments, egging the gunners on until they ejaculate.

There is one infamous gunner known to all as the "D.C. Sniper." As indicated by his moniker, he is from Washington D.C. The second part comes from his actions. He stands in the window of his cell looking out on the walkway masturbating while looking at female staff members twenty yards away.

White cars do not allow gunners on the yard, at least not White ones. Committing these violations invites detrimental consequences. If you're White, and you jack off to women, your punishment is like a mandatory minimum—stabbing, that's your mandatory penalty. No cop-outs, no plea offers, you do not pass go, you do not collect two hundred dollars. Instead, these sex offenders go straight to either the hospital or the cemetery.

The Sureños operate under the same rules. If you have ever been sanctioned for gunning at another prison, Big Sandy issues the offender a yellow card. It means the prisoner is a high accountability convict. Everywhere he goes he must turn his card in to the staff member overseeing the area. Each hour on the hour, the prisoner must report to the staff member.

For a Hispanic or a White prisoner, walking on this compound with a yellow gunner card is the equivalent of greeting someone by saying, "Hello, I am Sancho the rapist." Today, the Sureños attacked one of their own. There were allegations that he was gunning a nurse down at the infirmary. After a short investigation, he was stabbed over ten times. It amazes me that even being aware of the consequences in advance, people still head down that unforbidden road. Some urge causes them to try their hand.

Finding more and more that I have nothing in common with the guys in the car, I have been trying to spend as little time as possible around them. With my appeal pending, my days are being spent in the law library researching the law. Occasionally I visit the leisure library where I can watch National Geographic movies. People who are looking for trouble rarely look for it in the Education department. This is my new place of refuge. My priority is learning the law. No one is going to fight for my life like I will; no lawyers for sure. Making it to a lower security prison with less violence is my goal now. Being in this car is going to complicate that objective.

Today my insides are quaking with glee. I laugh at Steve. I've long rid myself of the facade that he is a viper. Chuck took a detour to the lieutenant's office today, and that left Steve the snake squirming. Steve had a thousand dollars' worth of heroin given to him on consignment. Chuck promised to send the money today, but now like David Copperfield, he disappeared with half of the product. After months of being used, Chuck figured things out, and paid them back for their usury.

Steve is in turmoil. He doesn't have family support on the outside. There's no one to reach out to for a thousand dollars. Chuck's Great Escape has turned their smiles upside down. Like an angry child he is throwing things around in his cell. I sit in my plastic chair, looking normal on the outside while laughing on the inside. Their scheme has finally nipped them back. It ain't no fun when the rabbit's got the gun.

Ready to explode myself, I make a choice. I can no longer handle this prison. I decide that I am going to leave soon. Deciding Steve is my ticket out of this prison, I begin to plot my exit. Sometimes in the morning he is alone on the yard where he does yoga. With all his crazy poses, there is not a day where he is not standing on his head. I decide this will be the perfect time to walk up and kick him in the face. When the time is right, I will punch my ticket. Steve is going to pay. I know that I cannot allow my anger to surpass my intelligence. I must make my move in silence. No one can know. Smiling in Steve's face, I play his game while I hold on to a burning passion to brutalize him. It isn't easy. My own life depends on being smart, and on leaving this unforgiving prison. I have to start over, reinvent myself at a new prison. Our car is spiraling out of control with a madman driving.

More and more often, Steve rampages unchecked. Mission after mission, he sends people to assault others for no real reason. Biding my time, I wait for the opportunity to lash out at Steve. He has gained his power through persuasion, intimidation, and playing off lonely men's fears of prison. I do not fear him, neither do I respect him. He has convinced himself that he has supernatural abilities. Shamefully, for a brief time, I too fell under the persuasion; his tough guy stories about knowing Whitey Bulger when he grew up in Southey. My stupidity makes me even angrier. The explosion is coming. Not just for me, but for all of us.

THIRTY-ONE

AN OLD FRIEND FROM DAYS PAST showed up in our unit after being transferred from USP Hazelton. At thirty-one, Pike was sentenced to a few life sentences for his involvement in a drug conspiracy in Jamestown, New York. Pike and I were the best of friends in pretrial detention.

After a mini riot between White independents and White gang members at another prison, Pike was on a bus to this concrete jungle. Some Independent guys hit an Aryan Brotherhood member named Pooch in the face with a rock and thereby ignited a battle. The melee made the USA Today after numerous prisoners were stabbed or maimed.

Pike knew the gang members had a plan to attack the Independents in another unit. Armed with this knowledge, he tipped the Independents off using sign language through a window. When the gang members made it to the unit where the Independents lived the following morning, they were surprised. The Independent car was armed, ready, and took the fight to the gang members. The end result: the White gang members were easily destroyed. The Devil's soldiers were left with punctured lungs, and bloody bodies.

The guys have been trying to reel Pike into the car. He is playing hard to get which I tell him is a good thing. I trust Pike because of our previous friendship. As we walk the track, I lay things out for him. I explain my plan to exit USP Big Sandy in the near future. In response he tells me that he might be in danger. He's worried about the White gang members. If the gang members find out that he warned the Independents at USP Hazelton, it might be the spark that sets off the impending riot between us and them. With Steve's craziness escalating daily, the battle looms.

I doubt Pike is in danger although we have to be cautious. It's good that he's decided to play the fence close with the car. He can use it as a bumper. I explain that with his troubles it might be wise to join the car. He objects. I wonder if my hesitation to make my move will be my doom. My grandfather had an old saying he liked. He would butcher Adlai Stevenson's hoary words. "On the plains of hesitation lie the blackened bodies of countless millions, who at the dawn of victory, sat down to rest, and resting they died."

Every time I pause my plan to attack Steve my grandfather's voice plays in my mind. I am so close. Pike should come with me. His next move should be his best move. The only person who knows what Pike is going to do is Pike. The holidays are here, and my immediate plan is to make it through them. On New Year's Day, I am leaving. It's the day Steve will become my sacrificial lamb.

Prison does not only affect me, it hurts my mother, my family. Calling home is painful as my mother does more crying than talking. Visits are bleak given the Federal Bureau of Prisons has sent me to Kentucky—a long way from New York. With the distance my mother sends letters of love and encouragement through the mail. I shield her from my pain, never telling her what this place is really like. My responses always are filled with promising dreams of hope rooted in the appeal papers. To die here would shatter my mother. I know this and that gives me even more reason to start over with the things I have learned here.

Corruption is at all-time highs. Staff members could care less about what happens to convicts. We are all despicable creatures to them. For the right amount of money some staff will bring in contraband. Money is the king of kings, the master manipulator. With thousands of dollars to be made for a few cell phones, and a package of heroin, some seize the opportunity.

People from this impoverished area have seen their fair share of corruption. Drug smuggling has been going on in Kentucky since John Y. Brown, Jr. was elected Governor of the Blue Grass State. Many important law enforcement figures, and local government representatives have seen the inside of prison as a prisoner. One of those was William Taulbee Bill Canon, sentenced to seventeen years on federal drug charges. Corruption seems to run in their blue Kentucky blood.

✳——✳——✳

THE TAIL HAS used the smell of cash to hook one of the country boys working here. He bought three cell phones and resold two. The biggest highlight for us in the car has been watching the Kim Kardashian sex tape. Myspace, and Facebook are also big things for us. I am amazed that this small phone is a computer. Technology has changed dramatically, making me realize how long I have been separated from the world.

Once a staff member is in a person's pocket, big doors can be opened. Big doors lead to big opportunities to make a whole lot of money. Like all of Steve's victims before, he has an agenda for the Tail. Steve always seems to ruin everything he touches. If he maneuvers his way into the Tail's action, he will likely destroy what the Tail has going on.

Lately, we have had a new guard working our unit. He is one of the few that isn't scared of prisoners, and he does not want cons drinking on his shift. Steve has voiced his displeasure about the new guard. Having him working our unit puts a cramp in Steve's hustle. If he cannot hustle, he cannot get high.

Steve's main hustle is making moonshine. He has the best hiding place—at least up until today. There is a steel wall behind the shower that Steve unscrews with makeshift tools. Today his product is finished but it's waiting behind the wall to be retrieved. Baby is a nineteen-year-old convict about 5'1", weighing less than a hundred and thirty pounds. Baby looks more like thirteen-year-old freshman than a convict serving fifteen years for three ounces of crack. With his small stature he can fit through the hole behind the shower.

Baby is behind the panel when the guard starts doing his rounds. Steve is panicking. He starts rushing Baby, urging him to climb out of the hidden catwalk. Baby is in distress. At Steve's ushering, he braces himself against a hot water pipe. The pipe snaps releasing hot water that burns both Steve and Baby. With no other recourse they scurry away from the shower, abandoning their wine along with the shower panel. The water sprays out of the hole in the wall grabbing the cop's attention. Staff from the building maintenance department respond to fix the problem, but not before Steve sends the Baby into the hot water to retrieve the wine.

Maintenance puts the panel back on, but bolts and screws are welded onto the panel preventing it from ever being removed again. Steve explodes in anger at the turn of events. He blames Baby for the loss of his hiding spot. Within hours two missiles are dispatched to beat the Baby off the yard. Despite all he did for Steve, Baby was assaulted. This angers some of the men among us, even some White gang members. Ruling with an iron fist is making people upset.

Now the wine has to be made, and hidden, in Steve's cell. His first attempt to side-step this cop is unsuccessful. The cop finds the wine and pours it down the toilet. A few days later the scenario repeats itself costing Steve money he does not have, and biting into his ability to obtain the poison that quenches his addiction. He threatens to hurt the cop, but like most of his threats, I ignore them.

The guard has been gone for four days. Steve was able to bring the wine to fruition in his absence. This time he was able to beat the cops. The wine is turned into prison vodka then it is sold to Adam, Preston, and others. Experiencing a false sense of victory, the guys forget about the guard manning our unit, and Steve's prior run ins with him.

A party is starting in Steve's cell. Adam contributes two gallons of liquid fire to the fiesta. The party is in full swing. Led Zeppelin's, "Stairway to Heaven" booms from Steve's room. The intoxicated participants pay no heed to the CO's presence in the unit.

Before long, the cop is knocking on Steve's door.

"I need you men to step out," the guard says, in a hardened tone.

Steve looks at him with darkening eyes.

"Step out for what officer?" he asks sarcastically.

"For a cell search."

With a crooked, drunken smile Steve replies, "Well Officer Friendly we ain't really fit for a cell search." The guys all laugh.

"Well, I'm going to search this cell one way or the other."

"Why do you keep fucking with me man?" Steve yells.

"I'm just doing my job, Steve."

"This is some bullshit! I got a life sentence. I'm just trying to ease my time," Steve says in a clearly intoxicated voice.

"I understand that Steve. There is no hard feelings. I have a job to do. So, are you men going to step out?" the guard asks, clearly on edge but holding his ground. This is the moment of truth. Whether the situation will escalate depends on who gives in. Steve bows down.

"Yea we're going to step out asshole. Let's go fellas."

Looking on from Dennis' cell, I see everyone exiting the cinderblock bunker with stupid looks on their faces. Alcohol and anger are never a good mix. Mix in a few life sentences and with drunk misfits, things can get very dangerous. The cop is playing with fire, and to everyone's surprise he is about to get burned, burned bad. The wine is found. As is the moonshine.

The alcohol finds a new home. It's flushed down the toilet. The gasoline to keep the party going has been discarded. This upsets the party goers. The officer also confiscates Steve's moonshining tools, wires with steel plates, sending Steve into a fit of fury. As the guard exits Steve's nest, he tells him, "Next time I'm writing shots, and people are going to be on maintenance pay."

When prisoners are put on maintenance pay, they can only make $5.25 a month. Men with no money coming in from outside sources struggle on $5 a month.

"So now you're threatening me punk?" Steve asks.

"Not at all Steve. I'm just following the rules. You should try to do the same. If you did, things would be smoother for you," the cop says and walks toward his office.

"What do you think we should do to this punk?" Steve asks his crew of drunk felons.

"I should go down and spit in his face," Preston offers. "Steve, let me go ask that punk ass C.O. what his problem is." In his intoxicated state Preston is being cheered on by his drunken comrades. He moves towards the officer.

"How about I breathalyze you, and send you to the hole tonight?" the guard responds.

"Why don't you try it motherfucker?" Preston slurs and lifts his hands. The cop pounces on Preston like a leopard, tackling him to the ground. Everyone is focused on the tussle. The unit comes to a deafening silence. Preston's pants have slipped down exposing his little, white ass. It's as if he is intentionally mooning all of us. The dayroom erupts in laughter at the sight of his white cheeks.

Adam barks out, "I have had enough of this motherfucker. He's dead." He's in a state of rage, a wild bull.

"What's up? What are you going to do?" I ask.

"He just embarrassed us. I'm killing that punk."

I follow Adam as he goes to Frank's cell where the knives are now hidden. Adam has knives in both hands.

"Man, I wouldn't do this Adam," I say trying to stop him.

"Fuck him, he's hit."

Adam leaves the cell. We all look on in stunned silence knowing what is about to happen. Steve's lower lip curls up on his red face as he gives

Adam the nod sanctioning the assault on his nemesis. He wills the gladiator to do what he will not do on his own. Adam jumps on the guard.

The guard gasps for a split second when he realizes that Adam has two knives with his name on them. Terror is written on his face as he realizes that his life is on the line. Somehow, he hits the deuces but it's too late for him. The first knife plunges into his back. The second one follows, hitting him in the head. Four or five more wild shots meet their mark. Leaving Preston on the ground, the guard scrambles to his feet, shrieking, howling. He's no longer thinking about breathalyzers, Preston, wine, or maintenance pay. Now he's focused on trying to make it out alive. Nothing else matters at this point.

Every man is out of his cell fully tuned into the Greco Roman fighting pit. My own adrenaline is pumping, my ears throbbing. My senses are heightened. The air whistles through my ears. Adam is pursuing his wounded prey like a wolf on a white-tailed deer. The hunter stalks the cop who backpedals hands out. His blue shirt is stained blood red. With a mad dash, he tries to find safety at the door. At just the right time, the door swings open sucking the cop into a place of refuge. Responding staff have saved his life with the opening of the door.

Shock has coated the faces of the responding guards. They see Adam standing before them with two prison shanks fastened to his hands. His long black hair in shambles, sweat dripping from his face. Adam looks like a warrior looking for his next opponent to conquer. It has registered that they are face to face with a man who has just tried to end their coworker's life. Like Fred Flintstone hitting the brakes on his foot car, you can almost see dust rising from the floor as staff come to a shrieking halt. Negotiations begin in an effort to calm Adam down.

"Adam, what's the problem? Put the knives down so we can talk," an SIS officer implores.

"That guy is a piece of shit. He's been harassing us for too long," Adam says through strained breaths.

Another staff member calls out to the unit, "Let's get you men locked in so we can sort this thing out." He delivers this in a smooth tone, asking rather than telling.

"Man, fuck you! Go fuck yourselves," convicts respond. The situation is on the verge of becoming prisoners against staff. They realize this is a delicate matter. It has to be dealt with appropriately. Other staff members have arrived with non-lethal weapons—bean bag guns, pepper spray guns, and other tools. After some talking Adam decides to surrender. He puts the knives down and backs away. I am overcome by a sick feeling knowing that had guards been forced to fire on Adam some people would have died. Knives would have emerged and transformed the unit into the Wild Wild West. There is no way that bean bag guns could save every one of the staff. At least seventy of the ninety convicts would have attacked. When it comes to the cops, race plays no issue, everyone comes together. In this place the hatred for authority overrides all else. Firing would have been equivalent to ringing a bell at a UFC fight. There would have been two teams, convicts against the cops. In here all staff are cops.

There is always potential for things to either escalate or become Attica prison in New York all over again. Our culture romances the outlaw, John Gotti, Billy the Kid, Bonnie and Clyde. Luckily, these convicts will roll with the situation. Adam's decision to end the standoff peacefully saves lives. Reality will hit him later; any hope of leaving prison a free man is forever dashed. His thoughtless actions will cost him dearly—another twenty-year term tacked on to his thirty-four years.

When a person savagely attacks another prisoner, consequences are nil. If a staff member is attacked a court hands down severe consequences. With people who are serving life those consequences don't really matter, but for men like Adam who had some light at the end of the tunnel an assault can be stifling.

Once the convict's patron saint/jailhouse hero is escorted out of the unit, we all locked in our cages. We're all emotionally depleted. The next day comes with a full court press. All cells are searched. X-ray machines are brought in to examine mattresses, thermoses, and other items in an effort to find shanks. The warden himself is leading the charge. Once again Frank takes one for the team—the knives are found in the safe, the fake shelf has been discovered. Somehow Ronnie gets a pass. Being Adam's cell mate nets me a full strip search outside of my cell.

I am shocked that when I am returned to my stone fortress, rather than the SHU. Steve is removed leaving me to wonder what I'm going to do if he returns. If he does, I am not waiting any longer—it's time to make good on my plan. My life is more important than the holidays.

With Adam gone the cell now belongs to me. Peace, solace once again. Alone with my thoughts I look up to the sky. The radio warbles in the background. Delilah's Slow Jams show plays and I imagine the sky opening up to a celestial landscape with beautiful, black stars glistening. Pearly white gates in the distance, angels come to whisk me away to eternity.

Willie Nelson's voice, along with Ray Charles's. They sing "Seven Spanish Angels," as I contemplate ending my life in this concrete mausoleum. Mental exhaustion has overcome me. The last twenty-four hours have been mayhem. The rain is beating against the window. I lay in my bunk asking God for just mercy. I am dreaming of a way out of my misery, thinking there has to be a solution to my desperation. Can this get any worse I ask myself?

He has shown up in my sleep, again, in the clouds, laughing at me.

THIRTY-TWO

ADAM'S ACTIONS ENSURED that we were locked down for a week. When we are released the Warden allows us to go to the commissary. During the lockdown I had very little food. Hunger is one of the worst feelings a person can have behind these walls. Hunger pains make me hate this prison life even more.

There is a knock on my door. Looking up I see Pike's face in the window. I wave him in.

"What's up Pike?" I ask, sensing his nervousness.

"Man, with everyone in the car gone, I'm worried about Dinky and these dudes trying to get me," Pike says with a frown.

"You're cool. We still got people, and them dudes ain't trying to do shit, bro. Trust me on that. We can still crush them."

"For-real! I think I am in danger with Steve and Adam gone."

Frustrated, I respond, "Look man you're not in danger. These dudes are scared of us with or without Adam and Steve."

Pike nods. "You got me, right? If they make a move on me, right?"

"What type of question is that? You're my dog. When they stab you, I'll be there to help you."

"Come on. Don't fuckin' joke like that Chad."

"Man, you scary mother fucker. I got you bro. We got each other. If they try to attack you man, I got your back Pike."

"Dude, I been dwelling on this shit the whole lockdown. I ain't trying to die in here Chad."

I take a deep breath before replying, "Man you're good. If they even think about doing something, we are smashing them kid." I reach out with my clenched fist to give Pike a pound. A formal way of telling him he is going to be safe. As Pike leaves my cell, I shake my head second guessing my own reassurances. He makes me think that the ABTs might just try their luck. We still have a deep car. Even with our leadership gone we far outnumber the gang members.

Ronnie has assumed leadership of the car. Not my first choice since he is a vicious drug addict, but I make no objections. Although I think I might be a better choice, as a logical thinker I can see that letting him take the reins puts a target on his back, not my own. We know Adam is gone. The day after the assault he was transferred to USP McCreary's SHU. The Administration made sure that we all knew Steve was being referred for the Special Management Unit (SMU) in Lewisburg. This is a new program where violent and dangerous prisoners are housed in cells for twenty-three hours a day. The program lasts about two years. Someone thinks this will change the way violent and angry men will operate. Incentives for good behavior might be a better solution, but those things are too good of an idea to ever happen in the federal system.

With Steve now gone, I do not have to jeopardize myself or my well-being. Staying here might now be an option. Staying here though, means I will continue to live a crazy life, but crazy lives are what everyone is living in each of the maximum-security federal prisons. Although some do have less violence than this concrete jungle.

Days later Dennis is released from the hole. He arrives with a "kite" from the Viper. Steve's kite instructs us to attack the gang members immediately. He warns that any hesitation could be the death of any of us. But Steve's power has evaporated now that he is no longer present. All of us, our egos are high and no one respects, or fears, Steve any longer. Everyone knows he has a one-way ticket to the SMU program. We laugh his orders off. Ronnie lights the missive from Steve on fire. It falls to the cell floor like a stubborn autumn leaf left too long, clinging to a desiccated, falling-in-December, shaken-by-a-bear, and snow-dusted tree. The men in the car gather around Ronnie and laugh with him.

Ronnie had his own hatred for Steve. He decides to send him a kite back. He tells Steve that his reign is over. He also calls him a chicken hawk—prison slang for a person who plots on younger prisoners for sex. The thought of Steve reading that makes me laugh. I can only imagine how angry he is, not at the chicken hawk comment, but at the fact that he no longer has the keys to the car. This is all he had left— now it's gone. The way I see it Steve's order was a last-ditch effort to exercise his power, power he knew was gone. Everything was about Steve. All along no one else mattered. Controlling the car was all he had left. He crashed it.

WE SEEM TO be coexisting with the White gang members. As long as they play by the rules. Ronnie has made it clear that if they renege, we will not procrastinate, we will attack swiftly and with fury. Although we are currently living in the uneasy truce between us and the White gang members violence has not ceased. Violence perpetually darkens Big Sandy's horizon. Today the Texas Mexican Mafia has struck. Emmit, a TMM leader, was attacked by lower ranking gang members. Two of his subordinates grew tired of their leader's drug addiction and debt. One man drove a home-made ice pick through Emmit's neck, the other stabbed him in the face, his arm, and side. Emmit tried to run. He collapsed twenty feet away, his blood contaminating the ground beneath him. The two attackers did not pursue him. I watched as they blended into the crowd. Some time later Emmit was whisked away on a stretcher.

Reality stares at me once again. Square in the face. On any given day

I could become a victim. I too could find myself on a stretcher carried away. It could be my blood left on the razor wire forever. The possibility of never seeing my mother, or sister, ever again disturbs me. It frightens me. Leaving this world on a stretcher, dying on a prison yard—neither of these are options for me.

It has only been four weeks since Steve and Adam were taken off the yard. For no apparent reason Ronnie has pulled a Chris Angel act. He disappeared today. Ronnie did the unthinkable. He decided to check in. On his way to protective custody he stole Tails' radio and headphones, along with twenty flat books of stamps. With only a few years left on his sentence I can only imagine he was tired of being here. Maybe the leadership position was too much for him. Our car is deflated, moving slowly on flat tires. There is no structure. People can see our car unraveling, becoming weak. We look like wounded lions now. Hyenas salivate all around us.

Pike and I are now a two-man team. His paranoia has caused him to make himself a stab vest. The vest is fashioned from a button-up shirt. He's sewn in large pockets where he can put books that he hopes will deflect prison shanks. A bigger shirt goes over the stab vest to prevent staff from noticing the protective gear. Pike has been wearing his stab vest for a week now. He has a job as a clerk in Education, so he has to go back and forth by himself.

Early this morning I noticed Pike did not have his vest on.

"What's up Pike?"

"Nothing," he says. "I'm running late."

"I see you not wearing your G-Unit vest today," I say laughing.

"Man fuck it. It's too uncomfortable."

"Well, I see you ain't paranoid no more. Thank God for that." I laugh.

"Whatever is going to happen is going to happen." He alters his pitch, mimicking the Russian from the Rocky movie. "If I die, I die." He says this jokingly heading out the door.

"I'll see you when you get back Pike."

He disappears into the crowd of men going to work. It's a cold

November morning. Pike navigates his way through the hallways, legal folders tucked under one arm. His vest hangs in his locker. Pike is unaware that he is being stalked by an ABT prospect named Russell, and an Aryan Brotherhood prospect named Pinky.

Once they are within striking distance Russell is the first to attack. He sticks a bone crusher into Pike's back, then rips it out. Pinky plunges another sharp prison shank into Pike's back. Both lungs are punctured. Pike's paranoia has manifested into reality. Three more stabs follow in rapid succession, hitting Pike in the head. He turns towards his attackers. He gasps for air, vainly trying to muster what is necessary for him to fight back. His attempts are futile. He is stabbed again, this time in both hands, and his face. A knife goes through his nose and lip. Pike falls to the ground in panic's grip as other prisoners look on in awe. Gaping at the battle before them, no one steps in to stop the attack.

Pike's hands go to his face in an attempt to deflect the knives. Russell and Pinky keep swinging their cold, steel knives. Both of Pike's hands are fractured, leaking blood. He kicks up with his feet at his attackers, fighting for his life, struggling to breath. Death seems to be inevitable. Staff flock into the corridor and order the men to drop their weapons. Pinky looks at the guard barking orders. His heart racing, exhausted, he complies. Russell follows suit. He relinquishes his shanks, opening his hands to let them clatter to the concrete. The menacing steel bounces off the hard floor, loud in the now silent hallway.

Like a wounded soldier, Pike stands up, blood gushing from his face, hands, head and back. Finding strength via willpower he rips his shirt off, balls it up, and wipes the blood from his face. He has the presence of mind to tell Pinky and Russell that they are both whores for stabbing him from behind. Somehow Pike walks himself to Medical where two, twenty-gauge needles are stuck in his back, and duct taped to his skin. Oxygen is pumped into his depleted lungs. Officials request a chopper to Mercy Flight Pike to a hospital, but inclement weather scuppers the transfer. Instead he lays on a hospital bed while Big Sandy medical staff fight to save his life.

At the hospital, the puncture wounds are tallied—twenty-nine in total. Both hands are broken, both lungs punctured, lacerations litter his beaten body. Miraculously, though Pike lives.

The hit on Pike was sanctioned by Dinky, and a California Brand gang member. Because our car had been so depleted, they took the opportunity to cause havoc. Cunning and secretive, the gang members waited for their chance. When that chance came knocking, they answered with violence.

Pike committed no sin severe enough to warrant the brutal assault. It all stemmed from that USP Hazelton incident—the same place Irish Mobster Whitey Bulger met his maker. Although Pike never assaulted anyone at Hazelton, he was nearly murdered for warning the Independents of an incoming attack. As a prospecting member of the Aryan Brotherhood, Pinky was selected to seek retribution. Pinky had less than two years remaining on his sentence prior to his attempted murder of Pike.

Most prisoners are never charged in federal court for a vicious attack unless another convict dies. This time though, it appears Big Sandy has had enough. Russell and Pinky are charged. Russell accepts a fifteen-year plea. Pinky elected to go to trial, was convicted, and eventually sentenced to twenty-five more years for the assault on Pike. His life fizzled out.

The cop is telling us to lock in. I have no idea what just happened in the hallway.

Someone grabs me by the arm. It's the Tail. "Chad they just hit your homey."

"What?" It does not register at first.

"Pike, bro. They just killed him."

I know he just said Pikes' name but for some reason I don't want to acknowledge it, so I ask him to say it again. "Who?"

"Your cell-mate. Your home boy. Pike, man! The cops said he's dead."

"Get the fuck away from me," I say, angry. My heart is instantly saddened as I replay what he said to me just ten minutes ago in the mock Russian accent. "If I die, I die."

As I walk to my cell someone tells me, "It was Pinky and that ABT dude, Russell." My mind is in unchartered territory. I close my cell door behind me and punch the wall. Desperate, alone, I know that I too am a target. Everyone knows how close Pike and I are. Since Ronnie's exit some of the guys have urged me to take the keys to the car. Other factions wanted just one Independent car. Ace has lobbied to be the leader. Both of us dislike each other, and I know that we need real leadership. In this dog devour dog world, it is either me or him. He knows it. I know it. What he does not know is I do not want to be the shot caller. I simply want to leave this bluegrass prison behind me. I am going to leave; I just do not know how.

The metal lock clinks in the door. I am alone. Again. I stare out the window into a silent prison yard. The sun does what it always does. It dances on the razor wire. I take a deep breath. Exhaling, I contemplate my next move. I know my next move must be my best move.

THIRTY-THREE

"Y OU JUST GOT IT Chad," E says.

"Got what?" I reply.

"Man, you're a leader kid. We all been selling drugs for years and never did shit. You got the pizza shop, the construction company, plenty of Chavos, and the rest of us got nothing. We all fucked our money up, but not you."

"We came a long way from sitting in the car selling dime bags."

"Nah Chad, you came a long way. You got bricks, and we're still selling bags."

"You're still my man, and I'm taking you with me all the way E. I got bigger plans."

"You ever going to stop this shit?"

"Let me tell you something. I hate doing this shit. People think selling dope is easy. Life's on the line every day. Motherfuckers want to rob me. The Jakes want to lock me up. This shit ain't easy, and it makes me depressed. The goal has always been to get out the hood so yea, I'm stopping this shit. This shit will always keep me connected to the hood. Who the fuck wants to live like that?"

"Man, I hope you never forget us Chad."

"Look, one thing I know, you can't never forget the people that were there with you when you were climbing to the top. Cause when you fall, they will be the people still standing there."

"Why you really want to quit? You're going to marry that chick, ain't you?"

I smiled at E. "I think so, kid. I love her man. She gives me a sense of being. I like the family thing, kid. Shit we never had—got to change that cycle. You don't want your son sitting in a car selling drugs, right? Just to eat McDonalds."

"Fuck no! Maybe this rappin' shit will work out for the kid. Keeping it real. I need to sit in one of the spots this week to make some money. I fucked my rent money up, and my chick's going to be mad."

"Man, them houses are hot right now. You're my right-hand man. I don't want you in there."

I pull a stack of hundreds out of my pocket, count off twenty-five hundred dollars and hand it to my best friend.

"Look man, you got to stop drinking. Learn how to do this roofing and siding shit then you can run shit. Legal shit, kid."

"I know man. I got to do something. I got a son coming."

"Check it out, I got to make a move. Got to pick up Rich and do something."

"If it ever goes down Rich Ross is going to rat."

"Come on, man. He's a good dude."

"The fuck he is," E says and opens the passenger door. As he walks away, I hit the gas, contemplating what he said. I chase the thoughts away, use the touch screen to turn up the volume—turning up that old shit that started all of this.

Smokin' weed in Bambú, sippin on Private Stock...

I laugh at the absurdity of Rich Ross snitching on me. We ain't never getting busted because I am about to quit. Two more bricks and I'm done. I nod my head to the beat.

THIRTY-FOUR

FTER A THREE-DAY LOCK DOWN Ace sends me a kite. We need to talk. He writes that after what happened to Pike, we all need to come together. During the lockdown, the administration rounded up Dinky and his gang associates along with the California Brand gang members. Ace wanting to talk to me is likely about his push to be the Independent shot caller. If I am staying in this prison, there is no way I am letting someone from Ohio, the caliber of Ace, call the shots for me. To do so would be to go through the same thing I just went through with Steve a second time.

The next morning, I show up on the basketball court to talk to Ace. To my surprise there are ten guys on the court including Frank. I walk up to Ace and shake his hand. I notice he has his khakis on, and prison boots. People going on missions in prison dress this way.

"What's up? I see you're suited and booted," I say sizing him up. I'm wondering if I should just hit him.

"Nothing's up. Thought we might have to handle some unexpected business this morning, but dude checked in."

"Who was that?"

"One of them ABTs. They hit your boy, so we were going to get him. The police forgot to lock him up. He got away."

"You were going on the mission yourself?" I ask surprised.

"Well, I don't like to ask my guys to do something I won't do myself," he says with a sarcastic smile.

"Oh yah. That's good. Lead by example, right?"

"Yeah, and I just kind of been wondering Chad. Like where are you at man? You got some of these guys want to follow you."

"Man, I'm on my own. Just doing me."

"Well Chad, it ain't going to work that way," Ace says with a nasty look on his mug. His nice guy approach has changed. He's attempting to assert authority over me.

"It's going to have to work that way my friend."

"Nah Chad, unfortunately it's not going to work that way. We can't trust you. You're from New York. You fuck with the niggers real tough, so we can't have you running a faction of an Independent car while I'm running the show."

"Who says you're running the show?" I ask, fury in my voice.

Ace waves his hands. "These guys say so."

I only notice I'm surrounded when Frank says, "This is it Chad. Dangerous time. You got a choice to make."

I am looking at Frank when it registers—he's not on my side. That's when Ace sucker punches me. The battle that I have always anticipated would come from my real enemies has just begun—just not with the people that I thought it would be with. In the end it was my homies. I jump back, hands at my face like a prize fighter. Blood trickles down my lower lip as I advance toward Ace.

"I'm going to kill you mother fucker," I say spitting blood from my mouth.

I hit Ace with a flurry of punches. He ducks his head in an attempt to wrestle me to the ground. I am able to push him back, but he has my long-john shirt in his hand. Ace pulls it over my head, blinding me.

"Stab this bitch," he yells, voice mushy through his bloody mouth. Panic sets in at the mention of stabbing, coupled with the fact that I can't see. In desperation, I flail out of the long john shirt. The first thing I see is Ace's right-hand man, Trago, with a knife in his raised right hand. Because I am moving, he cannot hone in to stab me. Taking a chance, I swing at Trago with a shattering one, two. Trago falls and I back myself to the fence, swinging at the men advancing on me. The knife is laying on the ground. Another prisoner named John Boy grabs it and throws it in the sewer drain.

Everyone is tuned into the melee between good and evil. I soak up punches from Ace, John Boy, Frank, and Coffee, while swinging back. In my position, the best defense is a good offense. While swinging I pray that the cops will get here, although a part of me enjoys this moment where I can let loose. Prison guards are yelling in the distance when I hear the gunshots ring out from the tower. Everybody drops to the ground but me and Ace. Just me and Ace for the moment— something I been waiting for since he first hit me. We exchange a flurry of punches. I get the best of him now and he stumbles to the ground. Thunder booms out again from the gun tower, but I cannot stop. Stopping could cost me my life. Grabbing Ace by the hair, I deliver three or more hatred filled punches to his face.

Somebody hits me in the back with a flying kick. It's my old friend, Frank. Everyone is back on their feet. Because I was getting the best of Ace, they have to defend their new shot caller. I throw a few more punches at Coffee, missing each time. A few more glancing fists are aimed at Ace. I bounce around on my toes trying to keep these filthy convicts away from me. For Frank's betrayal, I want to hit him before it's over with. We both connect with each other at the same time.

My adrenaline spikes as they move in closer to consume me. Warnings about live rounds boom over the loudspeaker, followed by a whizzing sound, then a bang. Everything is in slow motion. My heart smiles from inside—they're here, at least fifty staff members.

A big lieutenant body-slams me to the ground. It feels like Ray Lewis from the Baltimore Ravens just hit me. My combatants are all tackled. Now they're laying on the ground next to me. Coffee tells me I am a bitch, and I respond by spitting blood in his face.

Immediately the big lieutenant rips me up off the ground. I stand up with a smile on my face, blood rolling down my face, knowing I just embarrassed Ace and the car.

"You're a bunch of sorry ass punks. I just beat the shit out of you guys." The lieutenant tells me to shut the fuck up and whisks me away. First, I'm taken to Medical where some medical personnel stitch up my face. When that's done, I am taken to the SHU.

Ace, Frank, Trago, and Coffee have been taken to the SHU as well. John Boy evaded capture. Ace always said that if the cops were shooting at him, he would never stop. I find it amusing that at the first gunshot he quit. He got down on his knees allowing me to deliver punishing blows to his face. He was the first to hit the ground.

In his next battle, he paid the loudspeaker directions no attention. Almost a year to the day Ace initiated his assault on me, he was stabbing another prisoner on Big Sandy's yard. An AR-15 barked. The bullet exited his stomach, blowing his guts out on the bluegrass, and onto the dirt. The last time anyone saw Ace, a nurse was trying to brush the dirt off his intestines and push them back into his stomach. Ace took his last breath at Big Sandy. Like so many others he left his blood on the razor wire—gone forever.

WITH THE HEAVY-HITTERS now in the SHU, the gang members were ready once again to exact their revenge for the months they felt they were oppressed by us. Joe, a member of the Soldiers of Aryan Culture, and Danny, an accomplice from the ARM (Aryan Resistance Militia), caught John Boy in the yard alone. He was what we call "slipping." No one is ever supposed to be alone. John Boy would have been better off getting busted yesterday. Today he became the most recent stabbing victim.

Small in stature, John Boy was an easy victim. Danny dropped him with one punch. Once on the ground Joe stuck a knife into his body, soft like butter. In an act of desperate fear, John Boy was able to get to his feet. He ran like Forrest Gump. Danny and Joe gave an effortless chase, laughing a sickly, violent laugh meant to embarrass John as if he were not a man. John Boy ran right into staff's embrace, right into their arms. John Boy would spend several days in an outside hospital fighting for his life. While his blood was left on the razor wire, his life was not.

The stabbing earned both Joe and Danny a one-way ticket to the SMU program. Danny's gang brothers would later stab him at the SMU program. For previous cowardly acts, they said. His gang exiled him the day they unleashed their violence on him.

CHAPTER

THIRTY-FIVE

THE BATTLE WITH ACE and the guys has earned me my first trip to the Special Housing Unit. My stomach is in knots now that my adrenaline has slowed down. First, I am placed in an outside recreation cage where I am strip searched. Once that is done, I am given an orange jump suit, new socks, boxers, and t-shirts.

I am left in that recreation cage for an hour, pacing back and forth, angry, as my face swells up. With stitches in my lip, my mouth feels awkward. An SIS Lieutenant is standing at the gate waving me closer to him. He tries to engage me in conversation through the rust stained fencing.

"Marks, does this have anything to do with what happened with Pike?" the Lieutenant asks.

"What are you talking about?" I answer his question with my own question.

"Don't play stupid. I need to know if I need to shut my compound down."

"Man, you left me out here all this time to ask me that bullshit? To do your job?"

"You want to be an asshole Marks? I will send your ass to California.

Your dumb ass will be in Victorville," he says pointing his finger at me.

"Get the fuck away from me jerk off. I'm done talking to you punk." I point my finger back at him.

"Ok, pussy. You'll see when your punk ass is on that bus."

"Fuck you, punk."

I say this and turn my back to him in an act of disrespect. For a split second I felt like spitting in his face since he called me a pussy. My decision not to is motivated by the fact that had I done so, the guards would have likely beat me to a pulp.

Ace and my new enemies are only a few cages away. The same cop walks to their cage for a few words. On his way back past my cage he says nothing, but he does throw me the bird. I return his goodbye with my own middle finger, and a nice verbal "fuck you" that I hope he remembers.

It's standard protocol for most real convicts to refuse to speak with an SIS Officer. I never want anything in my file that says I cooperated with them. Keeping my mouth shut is observing basic principle. Arguing with the SIS cop, and not answering him buys me three more hours in the recreation cage. All I really want to do is get a mattress and lay down. I have a headache, my ribs hurt, and parts of my face are black and blue. On top of that my lip feels like it is so swollen it might burst.

The guards eventually take me to a cell door. To my delight no one is in the cell. This single cell was likely earned because of my refusal to answer any of the lieutenant's questions. They have no idea who I have problems with, or why. After what happened with Pike, I am sure they want to avoid anyone stabbing me. Not that they care if I get stabbed, only that they do not want any of the backlash that might come with it. With all the violence in recent days the prison goes on lockdown once again. I couldn't care less. When the prison shuts down most people are safe—both staff and prisoners.

I'M ONLY ALONE for a few days before there is a knock at the door. "Marks you're getting a cell mate."

"I'm not taking no cellie," I say jumping up from my bed and rushing to the door.

"Oh, you're getting one Marks. It's your boy, Pike." At the mention of Pike's name my stress subsides.

Two officers bring Pike to the cell, handcuffed in front. The food flap on the door opens for me to cuff up. Pike comes into the cell. He's uncuffed first, then me. The hard metal door slams behind us.

It has been fourteen days since I last seen Pike. He looks depleted but is able to smile.

"You alright?"

"Man, they fucked me up Chad. Not really man. They got me on these pain pills, and I'm still hurting all over."

Pike looks horrible, stiches in his lip, and nose. Metal staples decorate the gashes in his head. His hands have staples in them as well. Then he takes off his shirt and shows me his back. It is adorned with grotesque knife wounds. Each wound is surrounded by black and blue marks. His hands look even worse, as if they've been in a meat grinder. I turn away. I don't want to see anymore. I look out the small square window in the cell door and stare at the gloomy yellow of the door across from ours.

"I can't believe it Pike. They did that shit to you."

"Me either. I thought it was a possibility, but not this bad."

"They told me you died, man."

"Fuck. I might have been better off if they killed me. It would have hurt my parents, but they would have gotten over it. I got life anyway. This shit is killing them, and me, slowly."

"You got to hold on man. You got your appeal still pending."

"Man, that shit's a joke. They ain't never letting me out."

I am startled and look up quickly. The same SIS Lieutenant is at the door. "What's up?" I ask.

"I'm not here to see you. Where is Pike?"

I step to the side so Pike can talk to him.

"Pike, I need you to cuff up so I can talk to you."

"About what?"

"Oh, I don't know Mr. Pike. Maybe about you almost getting killed?" The blatant sarcasm is intentional.

"I'm cool. I ain't talking to no one. I got a life sentence. I'm not talking to anyone. I got enough problems as it is."

"Well, I'll tell you what. You want to refuse, I'll leave you in the fucking hole for a year before I transfer you to Victorville with Marks. Would you like that?"

"Man go talk to the dude before they try to get you killed," I say.

Pike takes my advice. "All right. You're putting me in a bad position, but I ain't trying to sit down here for a year. There ain't much for me to say though."

As Pike exits the down the range someone yells out, "Rat ass mother fucker."

I shake my head, fed up with the ignorance of prison.

✸—✸—✸

SOMEBODY'S CAR SLIDES under the door. This car is made from an empty toothpaste tube with small pieces of soap smashed down inside for weight. A long piece of string is attached to the end. This is the only way to transport confidential messages from cell to cell in the SHU. Cars and lines are also used to exchange money, to transport drugs, wine, newspapers, and magazines.

"What's up?" I holler out the crack in the door.

"Pull the line bro," a voice calls back. I pull the line as instructed. A kite is attached. I unwrap the paper.

The brief message reads, "Listen Wood, check this out. We know you're not a rat, but your cellie is downwind snitching on my guys. You can fix your problem with us by smashing Pike when he comes back. Doing the right thing can never be wrong. A rat is never right, Wood. You did good out there on the yard too with Ace, and the rest of those lames. Your own people turned on you, bro. Do the right thing. With Respect, Dinky."

I laugh at Dinky's lame attempt to manipulate me into assaulting my friend. Gang members refer to Whites as Woods. A group of Whites is called "The Wood Pile." He's trying to sway me with the Wood reference as if we share some type of allegiance because we are White. But if he had a chance, he would slit my throat. We both know it.

My written response is simple.

"Yo, check this out. Pike has two life sentences, and he ain't no snitch. He ain't snitching on them two cowards you call your guys. You made the wrong call on a good White dude, WOOD! With the utmost respect, FUCK YOU! And your PUNK ASS GANG! You better hope to God I don't catch you alone somewhere. To me you are a heroin junkie plotting on White people. Fuck your mother for having a puke like you as a kid. With respect, Chad."

I yell out the door for Dinky to pull the line. The kite disappears under my door like a magic trick. The verbal response does not take long.

"Chad, look out. Check this out, Wood! You're in the hat now. I want you to know that. The BOP is a small place, a very small world my friend. Now you're hit like your rat ass cellie.

My response is just as vulgar. "You're a dope addict, a bitch, and a faggot. You and your boys are the Heroin Brotherhood, a bunch of scumbags.

"Write your mother and tell her you're going to be dead soon Chad."

"Leave your knife in your cell tomorrow, and come in the recreation cage with me, soft ass mother fucker," I yell back.

"You calling me out? I'll be there Chad."

The other prisoners are hooting and hollering now. The entire range is alive. Guys are yelling at Dinky and his cell mate, Swift. Everyone is disrespecting them. Most of the Whites in the SHU were either beat up by gang members or checked in because of them. This is their way of getting back at Dinky. They kick the doors, making a racket. Dinky is being denied the opportunity to get a word in.

When the noise subsides, Swift is on the door yelling, "Chad you got all these fuckin' check-ins riding your coattail. Be outside tomorrow. We got nothing left to say."

Swift has nothing left to say because once he started to talk the other prisoners chimed in, screaming epithets at him with more kicking and banging on the doors.

Swift and Dinky are in the cell catty corner from my cell. I give him the middle finger in the window, mouthing the words, "I'll be there punk ass bitch."

Things have calmed down when Pike comes back up to the cell. I spend a few minutes giving him the play-by-play. Neither of us knew they were housed on the same range as us. Another example of the federal prison system failing.

We talk about what will happen in the morning. Dinky has to come to the cage with me. Once I disrespected him, he has no other choice. Win, lose, or draw Dinky must save face. He knows, physically he has no chance with me. So that means he will be bringing a weapon. Both Pike and I think I can take the knife from him. Retribution for Pike is only hours away—I am going outside to cash a check for Pike by punishing Dinky.

Sleep does not come easy. I am nervous, a little bit excited. Dinky and his gang have done so many violent, dirty things to people now it's his turn to feel some of the pain he caused other people. And I get to do it—I cannot think of a better person.

As the guard walks down the range taking the recreation list, I hear prisoners sign up that never go to recreation. Check-ins, sex offenders, victims of violence, everybody has an interest in what is about to take place. No one wants to pass up the chance to see Dinky get pummeled.

I am handcuffed first, then led down the range. For a moment I feel like a UFC Fighter making his way to the cage for a championship bout. Anger, and a thirst for revenge well up in my veins. I imagine I am walking through an underground hallway into a coliseum that opens to a death pit with screaming spectators. But it's just the lonely hallway of Big Sandy's Special Housing Unit. The thing I want more than anything right now, is to be able to grab Dinky by his long, straggly hair and punch his face.

The cold air hits me in the face, first. The steel cage in front of me glistens in the morning sun. All that is missing is the entrance music. Black Sabbath's, "War Pigs" would be fitting.

I wait hungrily for Dinky to appear. I see him step through the door frame, squinting as the sun blinds him momentarily. Anticipation builds. Everyone looks on in silence. All eyes are on Dinky, and me. My arms are heavy, palms sweaty, my heart is racing.

Calmly I call out to Dinky to let him know where I am. "Hey homeboy. Tell him to put you over here, Wood."

The guard steers Dinky my way. Our steel cage match is almost ready to begin. I want this to happen, need this to happen. As Dinky gets closer, he snarls aggressively, "I'm going in this cage right there! With *that* mother fucker!" Another guard hears him. Looking over, the guard screams out, "Don't put him in there. That guy is Pike's cellie."

I grit my teeth in anger. My face falls, darkening. Dinky made a scene to draw attention to himself in hopes of not going into a cage with me. Screams are hurled at Dinky immediately.

"Dinky you're a scared ass punk. You might as well check in now."

People are laughing at the comment. Boos rumble in from the dissatisfied spectators who anticipated seeing blood. They have been denied their moment of joy, in a joyless place. Dinky's credibility just hit rock bottom. When he was alone, with no one to help him, his heart faltered in the face of adversity.

Although I was unable to destroy him physically, I find some satisfaction in exposing him for what he is. A coward who manipulates other people to do his dirty work. This is who Dinky is, and always will be. A man who for years plotted on White prisoners. He blames it on the guard, but everyone saw what he did. I apologize to the spectators, an act of mockery, adding to Dinky's shame.

"I'm sorry men, that the tough-ass ABT shot caller over there in cage four is soft. Soft as grandma's toilet paper. Hold your ticket stubs as we will try to reschedule."

I raise my hand in victory, followed by a little shadow boxing. The people in the other cages cheer. Even the officers chuckle a bit. Dinky stands off to the corner of his cage dejected. For a long time many people at this prison feared Dinky and his crew. Today the check-ins who feared him most enjoyed a small victory watching Dinky become the fearful one.

Recreation has ended, and as Dinky walks past my cage he attempts to spit on me. The cop yanks his cuffs up pushing him forward. I smile at him. "Damn, Dinky! You're on some police shit man."

"Fuck you!" He hollers this over his shoulder.

Back in the cell I tell Pike what happened.

"Man, all them dudes are punks."

"I already know that Pike. Always knew Dinky was a coward."

"They need knives, and two or three guys on one person. Real cowards Chad."

"I exposed Dinky. Put him on front street," I say with a smile. Pike is strong enough to slap me a high five.

"Wherever you go Chad, be careful cause they are going to try to kill you."

"I'll cross that bridge when I get there."

"Dude, you might need one of them stab vests I made."

"Like the one you didn't wear?"

"Yeah, the one you didn't think I needed weeks ago."

As crazy as it is, we both laugh together. Today we won a small battle, but certainly not the war. The war is staying alive. The war is: continuing to breathe in federal prison.

THIRTY-SIX

IN THE SPECIAL HOUSING UNIT, days drag on. This housing unit is nothing more than a gloomy warehouse storing live bodies before packing the eventual shipment to a new prison. Anguish and loneliness have set in for both Pike and I. The SHU has a way of fundamentally dehumanizing a person, leaving them broken. The unit resembles a massive concrete bunker. The windows are painted over to prevent prisoners from seeing outside. It is a labyrinth of cells, halls, each pathway sealed off from the outside world by walls, gates, and guards.

The physical environment reinforces a sense of depressing isolation, and detachment from the outside world. It helps create palatable distance from ordinary compunction, and community norms. It is a place that builds anger while at the same time loneliness, and desperation. The SHU blocks you off from the world, and from the world within the prison. Some men spend years in the SHU, in isolation. Even though long-term solitary confinement is decried by human rights groups worldwide, our federal government uses it on many occasions simply as punishment.

Experiencing this living arrangement firsthand makes it impossible to fathom how any person can live like this for years. To me it seems like a slow grind of torture. Each day, little by little, a piece of me is dying. I am suffering; slowly being destroyed both mentally and emotionally. I spend hours pacing back and forth in a nine-foot area. When I tire, Pike takes over and does the same.

On our twenty seventh day, another prisoner is put on our range, just three cells down. Another White prisoner named Martin. Every thirty days Martin is moved to a different floor in the SHU. Martin stands in the middle of the cell and screams for hours upon hours. When his larynx tires, he lays on the floor, on his back, and kicks the door like a normal person would ride a bicycle. Sleep does not come easy. When Martin retires, we go to sleep as well. The whole range learns to get some sleep when Martin is resting. It is clear to me that he has mental health issues and needs to be in a mental health institution with medication, not locked in a solitary confinement cell in one of the most dangerous prisons the United States has to offer. They've left Martin here to rot. The good guys.

Martin never showers. He continually wipes feces on the wall, and on himself. A guard, nick-named Cowboy, enjoys harassing Martin. Sometimes he gives him the middle finger, sometimes he calls Martin vulgar names. When Martin is sleeping, he will kick his door. One day the Cowboy slipped up. He left Martin's door flap open after serving his meal. Martin had brewed an evil concoction—urine mixed with feces in a VO5 shampoo bottle. Opportunity how kind you can be when you open your arms to me. Martin aims his bottle at the Cowboy's back. And then Martin squeezes. His homemade super soaker sprays shit and piss onto Cowboy's back. Cowboy's instincts tell him to jump out of the way as soon as he feels the wetness pelt his back. Cowboy dances, a scalded cat. It's too late. Martin has struck.

"Mother! Fucker!" the Cowboy yells out. Other prisoners are yelling and laughing but none like Martin. His laugh is an evil gurgle.

"I got you mother fucker." He screams it over and over. Back covered in body waste, the Cowboy points his finger at Martin. "You're hit mother fucker. I'm going to kill you."

Cowboy rolls the food cart off the range. Twenty minutes later the Correctional Emergency Response Team (CERT) is on our range. This is not an emergency. There is no emergency, but cops are arriving, battle ready—helmets, body armor, a shield, and one objective. That objective is to beat Martin into submission under the guise of a cell extraction. One guard yells for Martin to cuff up. He gives the order three times. As expected, Martin refuses. Policy says after three refusals the cops can open the door and physically extract the prisoner.

After the third command is met with noncompliance, the cell door is opened.

Slow motion. Ten men charging forward tackling Martin.

The cell block echoes with screams. But these aren't the sounds a human makes, these are the sounds of a yelping dog. The Cowboy arrives. He slides black gloves over his violence-thirsty hands. He has the shirt he was wearing earlier. He balls it up in his hands. Cowboy decides to kick Martin in the ribs, so he does. Some of the blows are delivered to Martins back. The Cowboy is not finished yet. He grinds his old shirt into Martin's face.

"How's that taste bitch?" the Cowboy yells, quivering and uncontrollable. Then the CERT team hogties Martin. They toss him from his cell, with no more care than a TSA worker throwing luggage into a trunk. Martin lands face first on the hard floor. This makes a particular sound. I imagine not many human beings can recognize a human head rebounding off concrete just from sound alone. There is less bass than you'd expect. And less crunching. A sharp, quick sound. It suggests bouncing, this sound. I imagine it smells like wet mops. Martin is ripped up off the floor by his handcuffs. His face is bleeding. The two guards bounce Martin off the wall. They make a pendulum of Martin, slamming his face side to side, while they take their time walking him down the range. At the crash gate the Cowboy football punts Martin in his ass. Martin screams out in pain.

The guards take Martin to a four-point cell where they strip him ass-naked. They lay him on a cold, steel, bed-frame. He is restrained, each limb cuffed to the bed. For hours he is left this way, crying and screaming in agony. Martin's screams fall on deaf ears. What he did is the second worst thing a prisoner can do to a staff member. The worst you can do to a staff member is stab them. Shitting 'em down is a close second.

It does not matter that the Cowboy has spent months antagonizing a man with mental health issues. All that matters is Martin lashed out in the only way he could.

The prison tolerates guards' violence. This violence is silently approved by the executive staff and warden. In law, the correct term is acquiescence. There is ream after ream of federal court jurisprudence discussing public officials turning a blind eye to torture. Many guards hate us simply because we have committed crimes. There is a culture taught on both sides, a learned behavior. They hate prisoners, prisoners hate cops. Very few people in this environment show any compassion. When Martin hit the Cowboy with his squirt gun, the prisoners erupted in jubilation. When the guards finished punishing Martin, the guards laughed and high-fived. Together we all create a dangerous environment for each other for no good reason.

When we look at our prison system and compare it to those in Europe, the differences are stark. Switzerland focuses on rehabilitation. Here, we focus on cruel and unusual punishment.

No prison staff shows any type of compassion, or a desire to help or rehabilitate a prisoner—that comes with a label. To other staff that person is an inmate lover. In this environment this is not a label that any staff wants. Such a label comes with being ostracized from their team, their group. Prison guards have a code of silence that they live by. Very few, if any, would report the beating of a prisoner, or even his murder by staff. Anyone who did that would be cutting his or her Federal Bureau of Prisons career quite short. That person would find their advancement on the career ladder to be mysteriously blocked at every turn. When it comes to staff, what happens here stays here. Morals do not apply, neither does human decency. Martin's beating, and the feces rubbed in his face will go unreported, and in time will happen again. This is the world I live in. At least until March 2038. So many of us will spend the best years of our lives in cells. Decades will be wasted living lives of pain, desperation, fear, and hopelessness. The guards too have a miserable existence. They have to work in a hostile environment where tomorrow is never promised.

THIRTY-SEVEN

A FTER TWO MONTHS of this miserable existence, my case manager is at my door. She wants to talk to me in private. I am led out of my cell to the same room where Ace tried to chicken fight me. Through the plexiglass window I see the same SIS Lieutenant that I refused to talk to months earlier, sitting at a desk. As I enter the room, Ms. C. sits me in a chair. She finds her own chair. She speaks first.

"Mr. Marks, the SIS department has seized letters from the Aryan Brotherhood, and Dinky's crew, ordering you to be hit. We want to state place you. Do you know what that is?"

"Yah. You want to contract me out to another state. To go to a state prison."

"That's it. That's what we want to do. For your safety. This is what we are doing with Pike. The down part is you will be sitting here for a year, maybe two, while we seek state placement acceptance."

I interrupt Ms. C. "Oh, no. I don't want to do that. I cannot handle that."

"It's up to you Marks," the SIS Lieutenant says.

"No way. I'm losing it after two months of this shit. I'm willing to take my chances at the next spot."

"You could be in danger if you go to the wrong spot," Ms. C. says

"I'm an Independent. They got places where there are no active gang members. USP Coleman II, Lee County, Allenwood. Why can't I go to one of those places?"

"You can. We can put in a recommendation, but Grand Prairie does what they want. The people down there in Texas at the designation center don't always make the right decisions or listen to us. You're taking a chance Marks."

"It is what it is. I got forty years. If they kill me, fuck it."

"Alright, if you change your mind let me know. I'm doing your paperwork for a transfer this week."

With that our meeting is over, and I am taken back to my cell. I lay in my bunk, stare at the ceiling, wondering if I just made the right decision. It's impossible for me to continue living under these conditions. I am not as strong as Pike, mentally. At the same time, his experience was much different. Had I been savagely stabbed like him, I might have chosen differently.

THIRTY-EIGHT

L EAVING BIG SANDY is the only thing on my mind. A new prison may be my doom, but it also has potential to be a new start. This is what I hope, anyway. Getting out of here is never promised. Even the R&D department is dangerous. That reality is reinforced for me today.

Creeper, the first prisoner I ever saw assaulted here, was scheduled to be transferred today. His hands were cuffed behind his back, and he was led to the R&D department and placed in a holding cell with other prisoners scheduled to leave. Creeper was able to uncuff himself with a small piece of metal he hid from the guards. Prisoners call this, slipping your cuffs. Sitting across from him is one of the people involved in ordering the hit on him months ago. Slyly Creeper pulls a razor from his pants. One minute he is sitting on the concrete slab, the next he is running towards Chino. The look on Chino's face tells the story—he knows it's payback time. Chino doesn't make it to his feet. Creeper slashes at Chino's face. Chino struggles to get away. He makes it to the door, and he kicks hard to get the officer's attention. With his hands restrained behind him he tries to protect his face by tucking it into to his shoulder and burying himself into the corner of the wall.

Like a wild apache, Creeper slices up and down, yelling in Spanish like a man possessed. The guards respond by spraying Creeper with mace. Then they wrestle the razor blade from his grip to stop the wild assault on Chino. These two men should have never been scheduled on the same transfer trip. Because of Grand Prairie staff's negligence Chino will forever have scars on his face. Their negligence presented Creeper with the chance he had been waiting for, so he got him some revenge.

Chino is a high-ranking member of the gang that Creeper once belonged to. After his latest attack on Chino he knows he is a marked man—some might say a dead man walking. Like me, Creeper is in the hat. Kites will be sent to every prison. His name will be on them; marked for death. His only real choice is Coleman II, but like Ms. C. told me, Grand Prairie does what they want.

Some prisoners like living on the edge. It helps them manage their time. It doesn't matter what you get into, really. Being involved in anything keeps the organic mind from thinking about the heartbreaking reality that is being separated from family members, the world, and society. This is what moves men like those willing to accept an order to kill Creeper. Some men in here consciously welcome chaos, violence, and conflict into their lives.

✺──✺──✺

AT BIG SANDY, the new year comes in with a bang. I have spent Christmas in this cage, now New Year's. The prison is on lockdown. The guards aren't saying anything. This is usually a sign that something bad has happened. As Pike and I listen to the radio, we find out the reason for the lockdown and the bologna sandwiches from the newscaster.

"An inmate was murdered today at the federal prison in Inez, Kentucky. Staff members at USP Big Sandy reported that two cellmates were involved in a physical altercation that resulted in one cellmate stabbing the other with a prison made shank. The inmate was stabbed in the head, resulting in the death of the inmate who was serving a life sentence."

The dead prisoner's name and age is mentioned on the radio, resulting in prisoners hollering back and forth from cell to cell.

"Yo, Juice! You heard that on the radio?"

"Yeah."

"That was Roscoe, Slim. Someone killed him."

"It was his cellie, Slim," another voice calls out.

"Who was his cellie? One of the homies?"

"Yeah. He's from DC. Just came from USP Lee for stabbing a dude over there."

"That's crazy, yo! How much time the new dude have?"

"He got life. He killed some old dude who was a Pastor in DC."

"I can't believe Roscoe is dead, Slim."

The Roscoe they are talking about lived in the same housing unit as me. Knowing someone personally and knowing that they were killed here leaves me in a somber mood. Death is possible for everyone here. It could have been me or Pike just months ago. Living in solitude until we leave almost guarantees that we will not die here. We may very well make it off this mountain. Like all lockdowns, the one for Roscoe's death ends in a few days. The violence does not stop.

CHAPTER

THIRTY-NINE

ODAY WILL BE the last piece of violence I see at Big Sandy. It's almost as if it is a going away present. Problems have been escalating between the Nazi Low Riders, the guys aspiring to be California Brand members, and the ABT gang in all the federal penitentiaries. The Brand has issued orders to all their members, and the Nazi Low Riders, to hit every ABT gang member. Pinky never got wind of the order and doesn't know anything about the issues between his gang and his cellmate, Russell's gang. Swift and Dinky have.

Pinky and Russell make it into a recreation cage with Swift, just one cage away from me and Pike. The men exchange handshakes. Dinky stayed inside today. Swift pulls Russell to the side for a brief conversation. Once the guards leave the recreation cage area, Swift punches Pinky from behind. Russell moves in to aid Swift in the assault. Pinky swings wildly, backing up. He doesn't know why his cellmate for months has joined up with the ABTs to attack him. Swift rushes Pinky, overpowering him. He picks him up and slams him to the ground. Swift holds him down as Russell slashes Pinky with a razor. A piece of Pinky's ear is cut off.

The guards respond and order the men to stop fighting, but no one listens. Bean bag rounds are fired hitting Swift and knocking him to the ground. Guards rush in and spray mace on the combatants. The men are cuffed, then separated.

Pinky is escorted from the cage first. He walks past us. Blood is dripping from his face.

"Those are your friends, bitch," Pike hollers. Pinky hears him but does not respond. Through eyes watery from the mace that has reached our cage we laugh at Pinky.

Pinky was attacked because he is prospecting for the Aryan Brotherhood. Swift and Russell walked him into their trap. Being in the gang has earned Pinky twenty-five more years in prison and has stripped a piece of his ear from him. The ruthless prison machine respects no one. Seeing Pinky brutalized does give Pike a moment of happiness. He will never have a chance to avenge what Pinky did to him. Their paths will likely never cross again. Pike will eventually be sent to a state prison. Pinky will be here until someone kills him, or until he is an old man.

After lunch I am told to pack my belongings. I'm being transferred in the morning to USP Lee. I see the sadness in Pike's face, I feel the same emotions at the moment. With the time me and Pike spent in pretrial, and now here in federal prison, we've become close friends—more like brothers. Like all things in prison, everything is subject to change.

"What do you really think about this place Pike?"

"For real, I don't even know what to think about this place," Pike snorts.

"Honestly, this is the worst place I ever been in my life. It's a fucked-up life. I'd rather be in Afghanistan than in this fuckin' rat hole."

"Afghanistan?"

"At least over there you know who your enemies are. These dudes in here will smile in your face today and stab you in the neck tomorrow."

"Yeah. I guess you're right Pike."

"You're out of here tomorrow. Now I got to worry about them bringing me a cellmate."

"What are you going to do?"

"I'm not taking no one. Plain and simple. My life is on the line. I'll be in this bitch for a year before I make it to a state prison."

"You could take Martin, kid. He's your codefendant anyway." I say this laughing. Pike rolls his eyes, but he laughs back.

"By the time I get out of this hole, I'll be as crazy as your step-father Martin."

"Fuck you, he ain't my stepfather." I say this while throwing two playful punches at Pike.

Federal prison is an unforgiving world. With no remorse for anyone. The federal penitentiary can break a person. Like a machine it will chew you up and spit you out if you allow it to. Many men have left here broken, empty, destroyed for the rest of their lives. Tomorrow morning, I will walk down this range battered, damaged, but still alive.

CHAPTER

FORTY

I SEE THEM JUMPING out of their cars, my first instinct is to flee. I think I am being robbed until I see the shiny metal of their badges. It is the Rochester Police Department—narcotics officers. They rip me from the front seat. Rich jumps out of the passenger seat to run. The snow drifts down from the black sky on a cold February 4, 2003 night.

"Don't move. I'll blow your fucking head off."

I am laying down in the street face first, wet from the ground. A cop's knee in my back. I am handcuffed. Life as I knew it, gone forever. I never been to Kentucky, never seen blue grass.

BIG SANDY HERE I AM!

EPILOGUE

I WOULD LEAVE USP BIG SANDY and go to USP Lee in Jonesville, Virginia. On my first day there many prisoners from Big Sandy like Dog, and Spivey embraced me. All of us relieved to leave the horrors of Big Sandy behind us. Pike would later go to a state prison.

USP Lee had its own host of problems. I witnessed at least two prisoner murders at Lee, and numerous vicious assaults. Stabbings were common. I was stabbed at USP Lee. Eventually I would make it to a prison with a lower security classification in the Adirondack mountains. Being closer to home relieved a lot of stress. The atmosphere was much different, and I was able to get on the Education path. I was able to earn a college degree, complete over 100 rehabilitative programs, teach GED Classes to other prisoners, and facilitate Alternative to Violence Project Seminars. I also became a very successful "Jail House Lawyer," helping many prisoners win their freedom.

It wasn't easy living in prison with a forty-year sentence for a nonviolent drug crime. So many times I thought that giving up would be easier. I was never a quitter, though. Since day one my focus was always to get out of prison. I fought for my freedom each and every day. I would win other people's cases but could never win my own. It was joyful to win other people's cases and send them home to their families. But also disheartening to know that I may be stuck in prison for the rest of my life no matter how good the issues in my case were.

That all changed April 20, 2020 when Federal Judge David G. Larimer issued a decision reducing my forty-year prison term to twenty years. In that decision he said that he believed in my rehabilitation. I am forever grateful for that decision. I was scheduled to be released from prison on June 4, 2020. As I was walking out of the prison, a call was made from the prosecutor's office that stopped me at the door within minutes of my expected release. My family was right there waiting for me. They were waving to me. It would be the first time I could actually hug my mother in seventeen years, four months, and twenty-one days. But it was not to be. The government had sought a stay from the Appeals Court. If the court granted the government's request for a stay, I would sit in here until an appellate court reviews the decision that granted my release.

On June 25, 2020, the government's request for a stay was denied and I was released from prison after serving nearly seventeen and a half years for a drug crime.

Our criminal justice system sends far too many men and women to prison for far too long. While there must be consequences for our actions the time should not result in death by incarceration. It's never ok to send a twenty-four-year-old to prison for forty years. People have the ability to change. I am one of many.

I have always called my journey my Long Walk to Freedom. I plan to live my best life, while fighting for the women and men who deserve the same mercy I finally found after serving seventeen years, five months, and twenty-one days.

If after reading this book you decide you want to help others, I ask that you make a donation to the CAN-DO Clemency Foundation at

https://www.candoclemency.com/

Made in the USA
Columbia, SC
13 July 2024

38562669R00139

ABOUT THE AUTHOR

Chad Marks came from a poor urban community where he was raised by a single mother on welfare. He was thirteen years old when he first started selling cocaine. By sixteen years old he was selling crack cocaine. At twenty-four he was sentenced to a mandatory minimum of forty years in federal prison. He was sent to one of the worst and most violent federal prisons in the United States—USP Big Sandy. He spent every day wondering whether it would be his last day on Earth, and if he would ever leave prison a free man. He persevered through trials and tribulations that no man should have to endure, not even if gifted twenty life times. He took the same journey, travelled the same road many people who have gone from the streets to prison travel—chasing a dream—a dream to one day be free again.